the
FARMER'S WIFE
Homestead Medallion Quilt

Letters From a 1910s Pioneer Woman
and the 121 Blocks That Tell Her Story

Laurie Aaron Hird

INTERWEAVE

1 3 5 7 9 10 8 6 4 2

ISBN-13: 978-1-4402-4902-0

EDITORIAL DIRECTOR: *Kerry Bogert*

EDITORS: *Jodi Butler and Maya Elson*

TECHNICAL EDITOR: *Debra Greenway*

ART DIRECTOR: *Ashlee Wadeson*

COVER AND INTERIOR DESIGNER: *Pamela Uhlenkamp*

ILLUSTRATOR: *Sue Friend*

PHOTOGRAPHER: *George Boe*

Table of Contents

Introduction

The Farmer's Wife Homestead Medallion Quilt chronicles the adventures of an "ain't so young" Chicago city dweller turned Montana pioneer.

Ada Melville Shaw was an ordinary woman who lived an extraordinary life. If anyone could make the claim of coming from "humble beginnings," it would have been Ada. She was a foundling—an old-fashioned word meaning "an infant abandoned by its parents." The church records of the Anglican Saint George Church of Montreal, Canada, state that Ada was discovered on a doorstep on November 24, 1862. She was baptized six days later and given the name Ada Maude Stella Melville. Since it was estimated that she was two weeks old when she was found, her official birthday became November 10. There are no indications that Ada was ever adopted but instead grew to adulthood in an English-speaking Christian orphanage, in a predominately French-speaking part of Canada.

In 1880, at the age of eighteen, Ada left Canada permanently and moved to Winona, Minnesota, where she found work as a teacher. She later settled in Chicago, Illinois, earning her living writing fiction and poetry for magazines and newspapers, and doing editorial work for the *Union Signal*, a women's temperance magazine.

On October 26, 1894, Ada became a United States citizen. The witness who signed her naturalization document was a man named John Barber Shaw. Two years later, Ada married John, a Christian evangelist who was twenty-three years her senior. The marriage was presumed to be very happy but ended eight years later when John died on May 1, 1905. The couple had no children.

As a widow, Ada remained in the Chicago area and again supported herself through her writing. In 1910, the U.S. census records show Ada was living in Yellowstone County, Montana, with her friend Margaret Sudduth. It was from Margaret's in-town home that Ada would later relocate to her homestead.

While living on her land, Ada wrote freelance articles for *The Farmer's Wife* magazine and spent two winters working in their Minnesota office, where she was well-regarded. In early 1915, an editor wrote of Ada, "A very tender, loving message is in everything Mrs. Shaw writes. She counts each of you her dear friend and whether she talks to you through a story or the sage little confidences of Contemplation Corner (her column) or in the exquisite, fraught-with-beauty words of an editorial message, there is always the spirit of abiding love in her greetings."

Ada lived on her homestead for approximately five years until the fall of 1915, when she left permanently to accept a job with *The Farmer's Wife* magazine, in St. Paul, Minnesota. Both the publisher and editor (a brother and sister team) had recently died and her talents were greatly needed there. She began as a columnist and eventually became the managing editor of this popular magazine, which had a monthly circulation of approximately 800,000 during her tenure.

Ada retired in November of 1926, at the age of sixty-four. She lived the remaining years of her life at the Church Home for Aged Women, which was located less than five miles from *The Farmer's Wife* offices. Ada wrote her Homestead Adventures during the years 1930–1932, but nothing is known of her life after that time. She died on March 23, 1937, in St. Paul, at the age of seventy-four.

As a quilter and author, I will always be grateful to Ada Melville Shaw and the inspiration she provided for all of my books. The "Do You Want Your Daughter to Marry a Farmer?" contest, which she led in 1922, was the subject of *The Farmer's Wife Sampler Quilt,* the first book in my Farmer's Wife Quilt series. It was followed by *The Farmer's*

Ada Melville Shaw

Wife Pony Club Sampler Quilt, which features letters written by pony-winning children. The third book, *The Farmer's Wife 1930s Sampler Quilt,* includes stories from farm women of the Great Depression, and now the fourth book, *The Farmer's Wife Homestead Medallion Quilt,* shares Ada's own chronicles of her frontier adventures.

I have no doubt that for many years Ada wished to write about her experiences as a homesteader but faced the dilemma of how to accurately portray her neighbors, most of whom would still be living, while hiding their true identities. It appears she implemented a two-fold approach: disguising her true location and, to a lesser degree, altering the names and personal details of her neighbors. Hopefully, those measures were successful in keeping her secrets in the 1930s; however, with the help of modern researching methods, I was able to learn the truth of many of them. If you'd like to learn more about Ada's homestead and her neighbors, you will find a summary of my discoveries about them in the digital download materials for this book.

(Right) Longarm quilted by Peg Ries;
Pieced by Laurie Aaron Hird

How to Use This Book

THE QUILT

I made a 121-block queen-size quilt 94" × 110" (238.8 cm × 279.4 cm) for this book, but I have also included instructions for making a 21-block lap-size quilt 58" (147.3 cm). You will find general tips on assembling and finishing the quilt on pages 259–260. Fabric requirements, cutting instructions, and quilt assembly diagrams are on pages 262-265 for the queen-size and on pages 266-268 for the lap-size.

THE BLOCKS

Each of Ada's excerpts is accompanied by a photo of a block from the quilt. There are sixty-four 6" (15.3 cm) blocks, fifty-six 8" (20.3 cm) blocks, and one 18" (45.7 cm) center medallion block. Cutting lists and assembly instructions for all of the blocks can be found on pages 136-257.

THE DOWNLOAD

Downloadable materials needed to create the blocks and quilts in this book are available at:

www.quiltingcompany.com/fwhmedalliontemplates

There you will find:

- Additional background information about the blocks.

- Larger assembly diagrams for quilts in two sizes, lap and queen.

- Rotary cutting measurements for template pieces that can easily be cut with a rotary cutter and ruler.

- Templates for each of the 121 quilt blocks.

- Paper-piecing templates and instructions for all blocks except the five that cannot be paper-pieced.

For accurate printouts, download the files to your desktop, then open and print the files from there. When printing, be sure the printer setting is at 100% or "not scaled."
The 1" (2.5 cm) indicator on each block and template page will help you ensure the pages are printed at the correct size.

The Homestead Adventure and Quilt Blocks

Cabin O'Wildwinds

[81]

OLD HOMESTEAD

BLOCK SIZE:
6"
(15.2 CM)
SQUARE

Cabin O'Wildwinds was the very appropriate name I gave to the tiny something-between-a-shack-and-a-house in which I settled alone, a homesteader on semi-desert land with only the snow-crowned Rockies to relieve the flat stretches north, south, east, and west of cactus, sage, and greasewood country, not a neighbor close by and stores very far away.

"But how did you ever come to do such a foolish —crazy—thing?"

This question has been thrust upon me times without number by very sane friends who never could have been persuaded into any such adventure. I felt—though I could not explain my feeling—that I was neither foolish nor crazy; now that I can look back upon it all, I know that the adventure was one of the richest and most lastingly valuable chapters of my now nearly seventy years of life.

There are those who tell us that, definitely and inevitably, we draw our experiences to us and therefore each of us alone is responsible for whatever of good or ill may overtake us. Be that as it may, this much I know: From tenderest years, even while yet the child of a great city, minus any acquaintance with untamed Nature, outside of books, I secretly yearned, dreaming and awake, and genuinely suffered, to escape from streets and houses and people—to be somewhere free and alone with sky, sun, moon, stars, clouds, winds, waters, rocks, and a Silence of which I knew nothing in experience, but of which my spirit seemed to have understanding.

A Door of Escape

This hidden, perhaps inherited "homesickness" persisted in me through the years. The odor of rain-washed grass, the fingers of the wind upon my cheek, the soft beauty of a cloud against the blue, the mystery of a tree, would drive the yearning pain through my heart till the tears came, when, if not alone, I would be well scoffed at for a mood no one understood. Then, when half a century had slipped away and my feet still were strange to the delicious springiness of natural sod, opened—a door that led away from cities and towns, away from everything with which I was familiar—to the untamed plains that thus far had been the haunt of wild life, but now were to be invaded by homesteaders bringing with them their ploughs, their barbed wire, their families.

As it happened, this door of escape opened before me at a time when all other doors of egress from a rather bad aspect of temporal affairs had slammed shut in my face.

Receiving an invitation to be the companion of a woman friend, who, with money in her purse, had a gone a-pioneering for health's and wealth's sake, into territory newly released for agricultural purposes, I burned my city bridges behind me and struck trail from a Chicago boarding house for the Unknown, never dreaming how far afield the trail would lead.

[93]

RISING SUN, VARIATION

BLOCK SIZE:
18"
(45.7 CM)
SQUARE

Leaving the Safety of Home

[70]

MEMORY'S CHAIN

BLOCK SIZE:
8"
(20.3 CM)
SQUARE

The day I left my friend's home near the little new town of Nesterville, and "hit out" for my homestead miles across the level country, is graved deeply in memory—a picture of light and shade, of laughter and tears, of fear and high courage. I had engaged a fellow homesteader to haul me and mine out to the waiting Cabin up whose brick chimney no smoke had yet felt its way and to whose door no friendly trail was as yet beaten out on the virgin sod: my beautiful, intelligent shepherd-collie, Lassie; my winsome and no less intelligent little black cat, Betsy Bobbett; a huge vinegar cask for water, since I had no well and no money to sink in the gamble for one; my trunk, filled mainly with books; a few simple and essential furnishings such as bed, stove, etc.; a three-months' supply of food all canned or packaged.

It was anything but a "nice" day. Clouds hung low and the greasewood flat was dressed in tones of black and gray, a grim challenge to the tenderfoot and a very lame foot at that! While still far off I spied the Cabin, its new lumber shining against the dun background, looking very much like a carelessly abandoned pill-box which the wind would one day toss out of its path. But it was mine!

Unexpected Homecoming

With high heart beats I climbed stiffly down from the wagon, my driver looking at the house with a wise eye.

"So you're goin' to try to make it here alone? Some guts fer a woman, I'll say! An' you ain't so young neither!"

With feelings I cannot even now reveal, I put my new key in my new door and slowly turned the new knob. I was very sentimental about it—should have liked some sort of ceremonial. I looked in—I had not seen the place since the first stringers had been laid above the sod. And this is what greeted me: floors strewn deeply with shavings and other builder's litter, egg shells, bacon rinds, empty tomato cans, sardine cans, fruit cans, tobacco quids, meat bones, discarded rags. A mess where I had visualized a clean waitingness; stale odors where there should have been the clean breath of pine. I think Madam Fate snickered in her sleeve. Did she think I'd weep? For once she was disappointed.

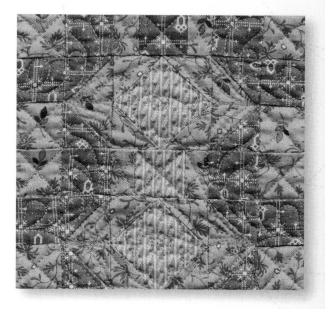

[59]

KEYHOLE

BLOCK SIZE:
6"
(15.2 CM)
SQUARE

Settling In

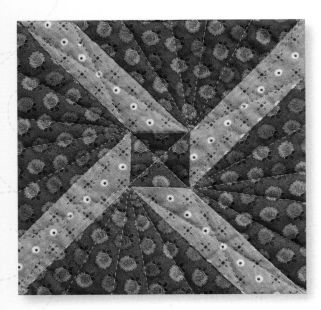

[5]

BACON PATCH

BLOCK SIZE:
6"
(15.2 CM)
SQUARE

My mover and I worked hard and fast and before darkness settled down, a stove was up, the water barrel was filled from a neighboring well, lamps were filled with oil, bed ready to make, boxes of food opened, coffee simmering, bacon sliced and waiting for the pan. How I loved it all! Then my first companion at the first meal in the new home drove off, and I watched him disappear in the thick gloom, which was fast settling on the land, swallowing me up. The only sign of other human habitation was a distant log barn and beside it a dreary-looking squat hut built of stone; there, I learned, sometimes stayed overnight a homesteader who earned his bread—since his land had turned out to be non-arable—by hauling logs from the far distant foothills. Aside from this, empty, treeless, lightless, pathless gloom stretched away to the encircling horizon. And the rain came down.

As a matter of fact—a fact I seriously understood later on in my mad career—that rain was a life-saver to the homesteaders on the new land, that semi-arid territory on which they had cast their lot. But that night, in my ignorance, I hated it, for I had but the narrow personal outlook—what was it doing to me! After all, it is that same narrow personal outlook that is the seat of most of our miseries. A year later, rain, no matter what passing personal misery it inflicted, was matter for the deepest thankfulness and joy. So we learn—so the soul is trained!

No Way of Escape

But *then*, I shivered away from the chill of the elements, shut the doors and locked them, albeit there was no one to lock out, looked around and whispered to the crass ignorance of me, *fool! fool! fool!* I did not like the voice of that coyote "singing in the rain!" I did not like the unshaded windows beyond which lay black, impenetrable gloom! I did not like the discomfort, the strangeness, the silence! I did not like to think that no matter what might be my need, there was no human help within call! I did not like to face the untried future! In fact, for a bad ten minutes I did not like any of it and had there been way of escape. . . But there was none—yes, there was!—a flour sack of mail picked up en route from town to homestead. Two or three books sent by knowing friends, magazines, newspapers, letters—a fat package of them. After all, I was not wholly cut off!

[41]

FOOL'S SQUARE

BLOCK SIZE:
6"
(15.2 CM)
SQUARE

The Light of Love

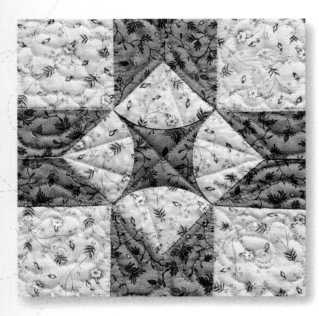

[120]

WINDOW SQUARES

BLOCK SIZE:
8"
(20.3 CM)
SQUARE

Clasping the material evidences of friendship and love to my heart, I proceeded to indulge in what women understand as the relief of "a good cry." Then I dried my eyes and began to read, and as I read these messages from here and there, one even from across the sea, my courage returned. After all, this was going to be all right! I was just tired. Blow wind, out there on the flat! I'll give you fields of grain to blow over, in time. And who really fears darkness—the merciful veil of night? There is a light that never goes out— the light of love! I finished my letters and the wee Cabin was filled with a glory that surely must have shone out through its windows to the farthest rim of the world. For love was with me and where love is, all is. Oh, it was going to be—it must be great! great! Great!

I sat thinking. The fire burned out. The damp chill crept through the thin wooden walls. Utter weariness took hold of me. I must go to bed. I looked around—bed? At that first slight move away from my letters and the friendly lamp, the happier spell broke. Primitive fear and utter loneliness again swept over me. Lie down in that unprotected place? Sleep—with those windows staring at me like the dark eyes of some monster waiting to pounce?. . . Many nights of many weathers and moods I spent in Cabin O'Wildwinds but that first night remains in a class of its own.

Morning Always Comes

So I lay awake, tense, numb with cold, quivering and afraid. Lassie, who liked the new home just then no better than I did, took advantage of my state of mind and leaped upon the bed, tucking her wet nose into my neck for comfort. As for Betsy Bobbett, who was half-mad with hatred of the "strange garrett," had not once permitted me to detach her from my person and now lay upon my shoulder with all of her claws hooked anywhere they might happen to be. "And the rain beat upon that house!"

And there I lay whispering to my flat soul, *fool! Fool! Fool!*

But morning came—morning always comes! There was much to do. I was at length a sure-enough pioneer.

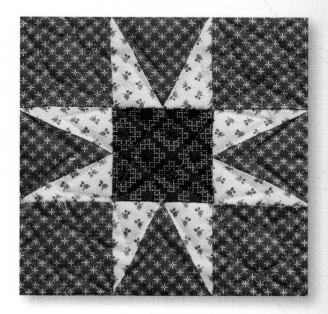

[104]

SUN RAY'S QUILT

BLOCK SIZE:
6"
(15.2 CM)
SQUARE

I Am Free

[101]

STAR OF THE WEST

BLOCK SIZE:
6"
(15.2 CM)
SQUARE

So I reasoned, had I not always yearned to be free from certain shackles and restraints of city living? Face to face with Nature? Well, here you are; now live up to the game! And there was a bit of mockery on the Old Dame's face. But she was right. I was free! Free to rave to heart's surfeit over star or snow crystal, wildflower or rainbow, racing clouds, snowy peaks, miles and miles of clean land, moon rises, star rises, sunrises, moon sets, sunsets, silence. Twice a day only the distant whistle of a steam engine broke the quiet. There was no one to protest or scoff when I got up in the middle of the night to stand on my porch and view the midnight skies. Or, feeling chilled to the bone, hours before dawn, to brew coffee and fry bacon and then with the dog, out of doors to watch the morning star lift the sun over the horizon while the mountain shoulders, draped in dusky velvet, ermine trimmed, glimmered against the purple night sky of the west.

For half a century, life—that is to say the organized, standardized manner of living prescribed by civilization—had not been any too kind to me. I had felt bruised, starved, deprived, cheated, but could not shake loose. But now here I was— free—a homesteader, a pioneer. I could work in my own way, play in my own way, learn the secrets of nature, do without what I could not get, enjoy what I had, read, think, shout, sing, pray, laugh, weep, without let or hindrance. I was independently alone with Nature, had all the absolute necessaries of life—with one exception. Water! The cup of freedom was at my lips, but the cup was dry.

Plea for Water

The barrel my mover had filled would soon be empty and I did not know where to get more. And even the bravest, the patientest, the most inventive, cannot do without water.

One morning, scanning the distant road through my good field glasses, I saw some men evidently at road work. I set out through the hot sun to interview them. I had to have water. I found a group of five, all busy with shovels and picks. They did not greet me enthusiastically—I suppose I looked as if I needed something and in that country at that time everyone needed something and it did not pay to be dependent. Moreover, lone women home-steaders were a nuisance.

However, I stated my need. Apparently none of them had time or strength to spare. I made it very plain that I would pay—anything—for hauled water. Grim indifference. I felt as if they shouted at me: "What did you come to this country for? If you can't take care of yourself, you should have stayed back where you belonged!"

One of them said: "There's a woman two miles up the road has a horse—she hauls her own water. Ain't you got no horse?" I shook my head and was turning away when the least-attractive looking one of the company, straightened up from his work and regarded me severely.

[7]

BEG AND BORROW

BLOCK SIZE:
8"
(20.3 CM)
SQUARE

Silver Dollar Knight

[18]

CACTUS FLOWER

BLOCK SIZE:
6"
(15.2 CM)
SQUARE

"I'll fotch yuh a bar'l fust thing in the mornin'," he said, "but that's all I kin do. Got enough of me own. Old woman, she keeps at me mornin', noon an' night about her damned bar'l. How in time she gits away with so much water, beats me, must drink it or water this here cactus with it or somethin'! I'll be around early. You be up—I ain't got no time to waste on no wimmen homesteaders!"

The next morning, at dawn, appeared my recalcitrant knight with a water barrel in his wagon, his well-fed horse trotting vigorously, the priceless fluid slopping out at every jolt. Gruffly he disclaimed my offers of help in transporting it pailful by pailful from his barrel to mine, and when he had finished and I handed him a silver dollar with words of genuine thanks, he glared at me as if he would like to kill me, pitched the coin across the room to my bed, let out an oath, leaped to his wagon, shouted to his horses and was gone.

But as the days passed, unlike the widow's cruse, my supply grew fearfully less. I had not neglected a single opportunity of interviewing such people as I chanced to meet, but no help came.

PART 2: AN EMPTY WATER BARREL

Borrowing Old Doll

One evening I was preparing my supper of canned tomatoes, the wettest food I had, when Lassie's bark announced a caller. Gladly I hurried to the door.

Approaching at a sedate pace was a huge, gaunt, gray horse mounted by a small, thin, ragged, fair-haired boy with wide blue eyes and a sensitive, even high-bred face. His air was timid, appealing.

"Good evenin'!" he piped, reining in the enormous animal and pulling off his tattered straw hat. "I come over to see could I git to haul water for you?"

Now I had been under the impression that hauling water—or anything—was a man-size job and this child, why, I wanted to hold up my arms, have him slide down into them, carry him into the Cabin and minister to his very evident physical needs—and mother him.

"You?" I asked. "Can you haul water? And where do you come from?"

"Yes'm. I kin do it." There was resignation in his voice. "I'm aimin' to go to school all winter an' I have to earn my books an' clo'es. . . You want water, don't you? A man told me."

"Why—yes!" Pitying amazement made my words come slowly. "I need it badly but—how will you manage it?" I did not know country children then.

"My grandfather says I kin use his stone boat an' old Doll here. She ain't no good no more for hard work, but he says he'll keep her for me if I use her right and tend her myself. She pastures on the range so she don't hardly cost nothin'."

[92]

RESIGNATION

BLOCK SIZE:
8"
(20.3 CM)
SQUARE

A Fifty-Cent Bargain

[28]

COUNTRY ROADS

BLOCK SIZE:
6"
(15.2 CM)
SQUARE

"We just had us a well drilled and the water's good and Grandfather says it has to pay for itself. I'm used to haulin'. I hauled all our folks used for a year before we got the well, from a spring 'way over yonder."

"And where do you live?"

"'Bout a mile an' a half over that way," gesturing into the deepening night. "It's more'n two and a half round by the road but there's a man lets me come through his place—he lets me let down the wires if I put 'em back right." He sighed faintly. Letting down barbed wires and putting them back right was not so trivial a task for such slender, ill-nourished muscles as his.

"And what shall I pay you?"

"I don't know," his clear eyes studied the distance. "'Bout whatever you think right, I guess. Would fifty cents a haul be too much?"

Chores Are Waiting

"All right, sir! Can you come tomorrow? And won't you come in now and have some hot toast and jam with me? It is good jam—I brought it from Chicago!"

But he shook his head, replaced his hat, and, quite with the air of a man putting temptation behind him, gathered up the reins. "No 'm! Thanks awf'lly. There's chores to do yet. I don't like to do 'm after dark but there's some moon tonight if it don't cloud over. I thought I better git over before you got someone else. Only way I can see to earn my books and clo'es. . . . You don't need to come down to the gate—I'll put it up all right—I'm used to gates. Good night!" Again that faint sigh. He was evidently tired to the bone—perhaps to the young soul of him.

At the gate the child climbed down—there was no spring in him. He struggled with the tall gate pole and the twisted wires. Wise old Doll sedately raced out to the road and stopped for him. He climbed to the high saddle and his thin young voice rang through the night, "Git up, *Doll!*" The darkness swallowed them up—the wornout horse and the baby pioneer earning an education in the wilderness. As I nibbled my cold toast, the story of Elijah the Tishbite to whom the ravens brought "bread and flesh in the morning and bread and flesh in the evening," recurred to me. There are ravens and ravens.

And water is quite as necessary as bread and flesh. The day of miracles, is it indeed past?

[75]

MOON BLOCK

BLOCK SIZE:
8"
(20.3 CM)
SQUARE

Paying for Schooling

[47]

GRANDMOTHER'S PUZZLE

BLOCK SIZE:
6"
(15.2 CM)
SQUARE

Hedrick was the youngest of three orphaned children who had come with their grandparents to the plains. The others were girls who hated books and helped the Grandmother about the house, gladly playing off from school whenever possible. But Hedrick had begged so to be allowed to study that he had been offered this way to get textbooks and clo'es.

Promptly at the time agreed upon, the little fellow arrived with his first consignment of water. The tightly closed barrel was full to the brim. Through the little square opening in the head, only a two-quart pail could be introduced. With this he filled the big pail I held and when it was full I lugged it into the house and transferred the precious supply to my barrel. For all his appearance of frailty the child worked briskly, assuring me that I was getting an alkali-free product, perfectly clean, meanwhile blissfully unconscious that at each plunge of his arm his grimy hand and dirty sleeve dipped into the water. But—what price moisture? Never have I parted with my fifty-cent piece so willingly as when I laid it in that thin little palm, and never did simple word of thanks rush home so warmly as his, the while, with huge satisfaction, he tucked away his earnings in a dirty cotton tobacco sack.

Water Don't Cost Nothin'

Thereafter, for many months, this little human raven of mine, illy protected from the cold by his scant and ragged clothing and as illy equipped for work by his scant and ragged strength, kept his appointments through all weathers and nearly always in darkness, for they would not let him earn his pittance until all the home chores—by which he earned his "keep"—were done. I forgot just how many cows he milked, how many pigs he slopped, how much wood he split and carried in, how many weary steps he ran while the child in him sighed unavailingly for its right to laughter, play, enjoyment, comfort, rest, and good food.

Once I ventured to increase the little sum per barrel but firmly he "reckoned not." "Water don't cost nothin' an' old Doll she pastures on the range." *Water don't cost nothin'!* To get old Doll up from the range, harness her, pump the water, lift the heavy pailfuls up to the barrel head, open and close the devilish wire gates—I hate the memory of those wire gates to this day—let down fence wires and put them back right, steer old Doll over the rough ground with cactus thorns ever ready to pierce the worn boots, for he walked beside the horse most of the way, dip the water out, then the lonely trip back, unhitch old Doll and give her human 'tending . . . *No, water don't cost nothin'!*

[64]

LITTLE RAVEN

BLOCK SIZE:
6"
(15.2 CM)
SQUARE

His Sensitive Nature

[110]

THORNY THICKET

BLOCK SIZE:
8"
(20.3 CM)
SQUARE

"Yep! It sure *do* git lonesome out here sometimes," Hedrick admitted to me wistfully when he had arrived one evening later than common, making his solitary trip in almost total darkness and through a wild wind. "But I reckon 't ain't no one's fault. When I'm grown up and have an education I'll have it easier maybe—Gra'ma says so. I thought I'd like to be one of these here writers for the papers—that wouldn't be so hard, would it? I'd like it. You'd git to know a heap."

Resolute and industrious to the core, the boy also had the sensitive nature of the artist. He passionately worshipped beauty. When the moon rode amid her chariots of clouds overhead, he forgot the chores at home in his rapture at sight of her. He loved to sing, his teacher told me, to read of beautiful things and places; he craved gentle amusement, shrinking from rough companions, though there was no shred of "sissy" about him; he loved order, cleanness, seemliness; he was sincere, loving, unselfish, dreamy, emotional . . . "One of these here writers!"

My Little Brother Pioneer

When it grew so cold that the water froze around the edges of the barrel and pail, turning his ragged gloves into icy mail, I bought extra pairs of warm mittens and made him change them frequently as he worked, drying the wet pairs in my oven. I gave him a pair to wear away but he turned them back with a wise shake of the head: "I'll wear them here this way, if you don't mind. If I take them home, the girls. . . ."

Whenever he would stop for it, I insisted on a big cup of rich hot cocoa. Drawing his sleeve appreciatively across his mouth after the last sip, and looking at me solemnly, he would say, "That there's sure good stuff—we don't never have nothin' like that at our house!" Then I would tuck his thin little scarf in snugly, pin the worn collar more securely, pull the old cloth cap down over his ears, pat his thin shoulder for good-bye, and, as I closed the door behind him, shout to heaven to do something about this and do it soon! My little brother pioneer!

[45]

GLOVE DESIGN

BLOCK SIZE:
8"
(20.3 CM)
SQUARE

A Poor Shelter

[2]

AMERICAN HOMES

BLOCK SIZE:
6"
(15.2 CM)
SQUARE

Cabin O'Wildwinds was planned for a home. The requirements of the law tied one to the land for not less than five years—I hoped to identify myself with my portion of the West for even longer than that. I had therefore specified and paid out my few hard-earned dollars for good building material and good work. Alas! Before I had lived on the dear little place for a year I found that all things are not what they seem!

Not all the tradesmen failed me but enough of them did to make my house a poor shelter against wind and cold and dust and heat and rain (when the blessed moisture came). The walls developed cracks, the roof developed leaks, the putty fell out and the poor glass splintered, the "select" flooring was of boards made from trees that had been well roasted in forest fires and very early in the year stripped up into a surface of splinters that made them impossible of perfect cleaning. I paid for good doors—they shrank and cracked until they were splendid ventilators. The little root cellar which was to keep my future garden crop safe for winter consumption, turned out to be a mere hole in the ground—the nicest kind of hidey hole for all the itinerant insects and small animals abroad, and the first consignment of vegetables, a gift from a good neighbor, froze solid. The only undesirable creature that failed to live in my cellar was the one animal which is a symbol of wisdom—the snake.

The Debt We Owe

What a debt we as a people owe to the pioneers—the land tamers—the house builders, who, driving the wild beasts before them, brought to reality their vision of fields of grain, the gleam of lamplight from dear home windows, the church spire and the school bell and for the cry of the coyote substituted the triumphant challenge of the iron horse! Sad for us as a people to take our vast cultivated areas too much for granted, forgetting the human pains and heroisms that bought them for us and our descendants.

[87]

PIONEER BLOCK

BLOCK SIZE:
6"
(15.2 CM)
SQUARE

The Sixty-Six Egg Gift

[36]

FARM FRIENDLINESS

BLOCK SIZE:
6"
(15.2 CM)
SQUARE

Nearest to my Cabin, of my pioneer neighbors, were the Heathlowes—Dave, his wife Mary, and a family of ten boys and girls—most of them old enough to earn and go away from home save when the heart-tug of their gentle, self-sacrificing mother brought them intermittently back. Dave Heathlowe pursued two callings—the ministry and the farm. He was good at neither. Although hard working, he was also hard-hearted, heavy-handed—a hard husband, father, neighbor. His young stock not infrequently died from harsh treatment and his "gospel" was as punitive as his whip. But Mary—Mary was beloved of the entire community. It was she who gave their huge barn of a house its magic air of comfort and hospitality, though actually it was comfortless in most essentials and there was but little to spare from the pantry for hospitable sharing. And Mary, pitying me in what she felt to be a foolish and certain-to-fail endeavor, took me under her wing. She cast about what she could do to help me "make a go of it" and the only thing she could think of was to set me up in the chicken business.

"Oh, you'll learn!" she assured me when I protested that I did not want animals of any kind about the place and gave her what seemed to me to be good reasons. "If you're going to farm, you've got to do *something*!"

So, on that memorable day when I moved into the Cabin, Mary was hot on my trail, bringing in her one-hoss shay, a shabby and old but still workable incubator and a gift of sixty-six eggs. I threw up unappreciative hands! I had still to learn what it means for a woman placed as she was, broken in health, poor in purse, over-worked, without companionship in her man, her older children leaving home as soon as they became sustaining, to select and spare for a gift of sixty-six eggs. Oh, how much I had to learn! Of true heroism, unobtrusive self-denial, sheer pluck, genuine manliness and womanliness. Since those days, when I hear delicately sheltered women complaining about this and that and the other, I can feel only pity for them that fate has spared them the grilling processes by which largeness of soul and toleration of mind are developed. Mary with her work-broken nails, her shabby clothes, her ill-fitting shoes, was a *real* woman—surely that is all that a woman needs to be in the final outcome of things.

The Unwelcomed Incubator

[67]

MARY'S FAN

BLOCK SIZE:
8"
(20.3 CM)
SQUARE

I installed the unwelcome incubator in my bedroom right beside the bed, for it needed twenty-four-hour-a-day attendance, it being impossible to depend upon the flame of the smoky lamp. For after all, when you set eggs to hatch, there is an inner feeling of responsibility toward the helpless, developing life—you must do your best by it even though later you slay and eat it. Somewhere I bought enough eggs to make up the one hundred which the machine would accommodate. But what was I going to do with one hundred chickens! I cried—for even I knew that they had to have shelter and intelligent care, water and feed, and I had none of these at hand.

"Oh, you'll learn!" said Mary again. "And there will not be one hundred chicks—you'll be lucky if you get a fifty-percent hatch—the machine is old and you're new. But fifty chickens will give you some food and eggs."

I could not contemplate even fifty with any serenity. However, I studied the tattered book of directions and a stray Government Bulletin on how to mother motherless chicks. And as the days went by I became genuinely interested in the game.

The Three-Room Cabin

That first week in the Cabin would have been one of unrelieved wretchedness but for two things: Much work to do and a head full of visions and dreams. It was real fun getting the little home into shipshape order although I could not help a nagging thought as to what I should do to pass the time when everything was in place and the simple machinery of daily living set going.

Unless, as in the case of the Heathlowes who had to have room and rooms, the one- or at the most two-room shack is a regular feature of the first year or two on the homesteads, with every equipment of the cheapest and most temporary. But I had another thought in my head. I had no less than three rooms: Living room, 12' × 10', bedroom the same size and a wee kitchen, 8' × 8'. And in the three rooms I had no less than five good-sized windows which I left uncurtained and unshaded—there was no one to look in and there was a wonderful world without to see as much of and as often as possible; my windows gave me five splendid, ever-changing pictures of which I never tired.

[100]

STAR IN THE WINDOW

BLOCK SIZE:
8"
(20.3 CM)
SQUARE

A Neat Little Place

[3]

AROUND THE CHIMNEY

BLOCK SIZE:
6"
(15.2 CM)
SQUARE

I had brought a lot of books with me and my splendid friends back East kept adding to the supply. In the four available corners of living room and kitchen, I had shelves running from floor to ceiling, and the carpenter managed to wrangle a small closet beside the brick chimney so that I was the envy of women who had "no place to put anything," causing a general reign of disorder about them. My "wee bit hoosie" I managed to keep as tidy as a model house in a department store plus a decided homeness which appealed to my occasional visitors—especially men who came to work for me. "You sure got a neat little place here," quoth one bachelor. "Not thinkin' of gettin' married, be you?" My assurance on that head was so clear and so positive that the question was never raised again.

Besides my books I had a good field glass, a good microscope, a typewriter and a sewing machine. The microscope and the typewriter were noted with something like scorn—what did you do with such contraptions on a *farm*? "But then she ain's goin' to farm none—she'll up an' hike out o' here the first time the thermometer goes out o' sight."

On the building papered-walls I had some good prints, a map of the United States, a world map—for there was always a ferment in the Balkans and I'd like to keep posted, a map of the State and a map of my quarter-section. But no calendar. This was a mistake as you will presently see. Outside, I had a thermometer—would the mercury go out of sight? Oh well, I meant to stick!

Gumbo Land

So while the rain came down during that first week of testing, I created my home and, on paper, laid out my first garden. I already had an enormous package of seeds which I had ordered late in the winter. I'd show these scoffers who wondered what "that there old woman thought she was a-doin' on a homestead!"

But despite all my resolutions to the contrary, that week and many weeks that followed tested my courage to the bottom. For one thing there was the gumbo*. No one had told me mine was gumbo land and if they had I should have been none the wiser. Very soon my new floors and my very new thoughts were "sicklied o'er" with the sticky grey "cast" of gumbo. Both cat and dog showed their hatred of it—I had to soak their poor paws in warm water—and I could illy spare water for such purposes—to relieve them of the misery of the adhesive mass that daily got between their toes. For the first time in my life I was completely out of touch with humanity and for day following day could not discover on the distant road even a passing horseman. The stillness punctured only by the steady drip of the rain—I was not yet wise enough to be thanking God for that fall of moisture, the howl of the wind and the night song of the coyotes stretched my nerves to the twanging point and I said to myself, "If I feel like this now, what is going to happen to me in the five years ahead?" And once again I would whisper to my humiliation: *Oh, fool! Fool! Fool!*

* Colloquial expression for soil that is challenging to work due to high silt or clay content.

[44]

GARDEN PATHS

BLOCK SIZE:
8"
(20.3 CM)
SQUARE

Glory Be!

[91]

RAINBOW BLOCK

BLOCK SIZE:
6"
(15.2 CM)
SQUARE

Then came the rainbow. A rainbow that has sent its heavenly glory through the years that have passed since it faded from earthly sight!

It was at the end of the first week in the Cabin. There was a sudden lightening of the persistent gloom. For the thousandth time I went out on my porch—*glory be*! The clouds were breaking away. The rain had almost ceased. And over yonder, yet so close as to seem almost within reach of my hand, was a rainbow and such a rainbow as my city-hindered vision had never dreamed could be. Stretched entirely across the dome of the sky, its broad bands of pulsating color jewel-clear against the soft grey background of clouds, was the marvelous "token of the ancient covenant." And at the base of either arch, there spread back on the wet earth for miles, a glowing reflection of the arch in the sky. It was unbelievable, unearthly, soul-shaking. While I held my breath, watching, the secondary bow appeared, scarcely less brilliant than the original, and after that even a third lovely dim replica.

My Bow in the Clouds

All of this which I have struggled to describe, was in itself enough to shine away my gloom but there was yet a crowning touch. Straight before me and directly beneath the center of the main arch, there came into view a distant homesteader's shack, a lowly house indeed, and in its window shone a light, the ray from a common kerosene lamp—but a beam that came straight across the miles to me, like a living beacon of promise from the ancient Book:

"The heavens declare the glory of God and the firmament showeth his handiwork. . . . Day unto day uttereth speech and night unto night showeth knowledge. . . . The earth is the Lord's and the fullness thereof. . . . He is the King of Glory! . . . I have set my bow in the clouds . . . . the everlasting covenant between God and every living thing. . . ."

[6]

BEACON LIGHTS

BLOCK SIZE:
6"
(15.2 CM)
SQUARE

Wee Yellow Miracles

[76]

MOTHER HEN

BLOCK SIZE:
8"
(20.3 CM)
SQUARE

While the gumbo dried, while faint hints of green illuminated the dun of the sod, while the greasewood slowly put out its salty green spikes, I kept on keeping incubator. The silent machine really grew eloquent to me. Would the twenty-one days never be fulfilled? And what should I do with one hundred motherless chicks?

Then, one night, Lassie aroused me out of a sound sleep—leaping up on my bed, a forbidden luxury, and pawing me in frantic excitement. My first thought was robbers—someone breaking in. Then I heard it: *Cheep! Cheep! Cheep!* That life had not been there a few hours before—a miracle! I gently took the lone wee yellow thing out and to Lassie's huge discomfiture, cuddled it beneath my chin. *My* chicken! But it did not seem to appreciate my human hovering so I replaced it and then, overcome by a vision of myself in new character, collapsed on the bed in gales of semi-hysterical laughter: There I was, erstwhile city business woman, transformed into a veritable old hen fussily bringing off her first brood.

By morning there were sixteen lusty chirpers but after that the miracle ceased working. I was in despair. The bulletin which I had studied carefully, had something to the effect that if for various mysterious reasons, the birds did not pip the shells at the given time, there were Caesarian tactics that could be employed to set them free of their prison.

All remaining silent in the incubator I rolled up my sleeves
and went unwillingly to work. . . . Those who know chickens
do not need to have me explain further—those who do not,
are well spared. . . . 'Twas a horrid scene! Endeavoring to save
life, I slew! And when my heroic endeavors were concluded,
I still had but the sixteen original cheepers to the good.
I called anathema down on Mary's innocent head and was
sure I should never be able to eat another egg so long as
I should live.

Vain Endeavors

[117]

WATCHING THE CALENDAR

BLOCK SIZE:
8"
(20.3 CM)
SQUARE

Now Mary had been watching the calendar and when the chicks were about three days old came to see how we had fared. She gasped at the small family. Then she comforted me. Doubtless I had done something contrary to or had not done something according to Nature. Next time would be an improvement. Then we chatted about this and that and in some connection the day of the week was named. "But this is not Wednesday!" I corrected her. "Oh, but it is. Dave preached on Sunday. On Monday I washed—yesterday, Tuesday, I finished up all my ironing so I could get off to see you this afternoon."

I did some thinking. Then a great light broke in upon me. For some occult reason those sixteen birds had arrived at the first possible moment, but due to rain and loneliness and depression, I had lost count of a day and had performed my Caesarian operations too soon—perhaps it would have been a one-hundred-percent hatch after all. I fairly wept. But Mary went off into gales of laughter until she too had tears on her face. The old wooden hen had done her smoky best. She had needed only a little more time.

Heaven to Be Alone

Mary patted my cheek comfortingly as, after a cup of tea, she climbed into her rickety old gig and turned the mare homeward. "I'll send one of the boys over tomorrow with a good big calendar," she said. "It's about the only thing you haven't got—except experience. Don't let yourself get lonesome. You know—only don't tell anyone—I'm the preacher's wife and it wouldn't do—I'd give all I've got and some years of my life to change places with you! Wouldn't it be heaven to be alone—to read and rest and think and write to my old friends and loaf and do my hair and keep my nails pretty, and get acquainted with myself once more! But I guess it'll be just work, work, work, to the end."

It was when the chicks were about two weeks old and could still be kept under my eye in their moveable box that the Episode of the Cake took place.

[54]

HOUSEWIFE'S DREAM

BLOCK SIZE:
8"
(20.3 CM)
SQUARE

A Failed Business

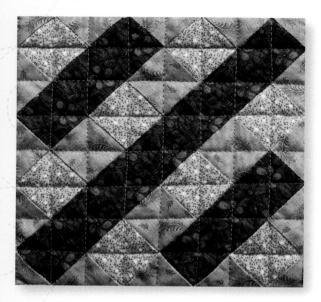

[90]

RAILROAD CROSSING

BLOCK SIZE:
6"
(15.2 CM)
SQUARE

All sorts and conditions of folk took up homesteads. Among the many whom I met was a tired-out court stenographer who came in search of health more than dollars. She was full of enthusiasm and poetry and plans when I first saw her—but a conquered woman when she drove from my Cabin door en route for an east bound Pullman train.

In some way she had acquired great skill in making cake and brought with her when she came stores of spices, flavoring extracts, raisins, currants, citron, nuts, coloring matter, what not. She had a horse and small cart and proposed to make up the cakes in batches and then drive leisurely from home to home, selling them to housewives who were too busy or too ignorant to bake good cake for their families. It was a lovely scheme. She would have employment, come in touch with the people and turn an honest dollar while waiting for her first wheat crop to come in. But she never had lived alone. So, when the winds blew and the coyotes howled and the cactus annoyed and the snake affrighted and the silence and loneliness bored deeply, her courage seeped out and was no more. As soon as possible she took advantage of the provision whereby $400 could be substituted for residence on the land, packed her trunk and fled for the comfortable city and a good job. There were other ways of regaining health! The entire contents of her cake pantry she donated to me because I had stayed with her through one night of illness that would have been more difficult than it was had she been alone.

Keeping the Blues Away

One day when I was wondering precisely what to do next—as it was too early for out-of-door work—to keep the blues at a distance, it occurred to me that I would make a cake, a very special kind of cake and dividing it into sizable portions give it to several of my homesteading women comrades who at one time and another had been particularly kind to me in my lonely estate. In my trunk was a very old and greatly treasured recipe book, that over a period of long years and via sailing vessel, steamboat, train, carriage, wagon, had come from Derby, England, even to lowly Cabin O'Wildwinds. In it was a black fruit cake recipe that was far more than a century old—copied there by a young housekeeper who had it from her ancestors. At home we children always called it The Cake pronouncing the common words with a touch of awe. For this was no common cake. It was eaten only on state and family occasions: The Queen's birthday, a christening day, on New Year's day, at Christmas time, always at family weddings.

[111]

TREASURED RECIPE

BLOCK SIZE:
6"
(15.2 CM)
SQUARE

The Aroma of Home

I decided to make The Cake in quantity enough to fill my largest bakepan. I had stores of tissue paper and bright ribbons in my trunk. And I would compose a jingle setting forth the history of the recipe. It would be, if not a gift of much monetary value, something that would tell my friends my thoughts of them and bring a wee note of unusual interest into their humdrum days. I went to work.

It took me practically all of two days steady work to prepare the fruit and nuts and compound all the ingredients as I knew they should be compounded. The morning of the third day I baked it. The result was perfect save that the aroma stealing out of the oven gave me as sharp a turn of homesickness as I shall ever experience in this life! But that didn't matter. When The Cake was cold I set it carefully away to ripen for a week or two before cutting it.

[112]

TWISTED RIBBON

BLOCK SIZE:
8"
(20.3 CM)
SQUARE

Saint Mary Bringing Quilts

Then I came down with a severe cold and when Hedrick, my faithful Knight of the Water Barrel, came with his customary consignment, I could not speak aloud. Quiet though he was, the boy had caught the trick of friendly gossip and, meeting one of the Heathlowe boys on his trail home, told him of my state and a few hours later, here came Saint Mary with the one-hoss shay and all the blankets and quilts off her beds to carry me back with her and be nursed back to normal. The invitation was most alluring, although I knew her to be overworked and the home overcrowded.

"But what about the chickens!" I exclaimed. Already my family of livestock was beginning to impose restraint on my movements.

"We'll just take them along too. We'll put a big dish of food where the cat can get to it—she'll stick to the house till you come back—and Lassie can have one final fight with our dogs and settle the business once and for all. You can't stay here alone and that's flat—not while there's room under my roof!"

So we departed. But while I was gathering up my things, I thought of The Cake. Why not give it as it was to Mary? How good she had been to me! How little of color there was in her life! No leisure and practically no pleasure. She could store it away in her cellar and when her many callers came—being a preacher's wife with her house by the side of the road she had a sufficiency of "company" she would have something for a real treat all winter long. A cake that size would serve many people for months! So I wrapped it up carefully in snowy cloths and slipped it into the back of the shay without her noticing.

[43]

FRIENDSHIP QUILT

BLOCK SIZE:
8"
(20.3 CM)
SQUARE

Treats Snatched Away

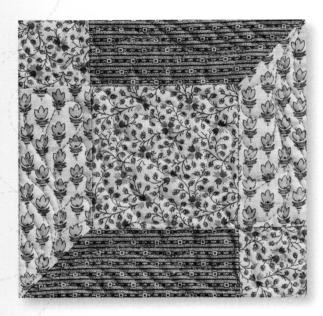

[26]

COMPANY CAKE

BLOCK SIZE:
6"
(15.2 CM)
SQUARE

When we reached the house, I took the cake to her in the kitchen and explained what it was and why I had made it—making very clear to her that it was no common cake to be served in quantity or at any time. Her oldest daughter, a tall, always-hungry, discontented young woman, was standing by as I spoke.

"For company?" she asked, taking the bundle unopened from her mother's hands. "Here's company right now—you'll never have better!" Therewith she deftly but not deferentially stripped The Cake of its wrappings, snatched up a huge butcher knife with which the mother had been slicing bacon, hacked off a thick crooked slice and walked off munching. Mary looked at me with a smothered sigh, dropped a cloth over The Cake and drew me out of the kitchen. I reflecting the while that just so were treats snatched from her.

That evening we sat fifteen around the crowded table—twelve of the family, myself and two men who were out claim hunting and managed to drop in at meal time. There was the usual farm-home meal: bread and butter, milk, fried potatoes, fried eggs, bacon, coffee, and—heaped up on two common plates, The Cake, cut in hunks and chunks. The refined cake-soul of me shuddered. Said the youngest boy, a starved-looking gangling of nine, as he crammed the last of his second hunk into his mouth and with an eye on his mother reached a stealthy paw for a third, "Say, Maw! Ask her to show you how to make this. It's lots nicer'n what you make!"

Offerings of Kindness

In the far past, The Cake's aroma suggested feast days and memorable occasions, with all accompaniments of formal dress and behavior. Now, should it greet my nostrils, it would bring back the never-to-be-forgotten flavor of the Great Plains with keen and tender remembrance of informal but down-to-the-bone hospitality that meant the shared life, the divided burden, the reinforced courage. For a week, three hard-working daughters of a harder-working pioneer mother slept on quilts spread on the floor so that the mother's elderly guest should have a comfortable bed by herself. And there were hot flatirons and hot drinks and milk toasts and fires kept up and heart offerings of kindness and cordiality. What matter sacrosanct cake? What price friendship? After all, I reflected it is *folks* that count and character—the little surface mistakes may well be regarded as the earmarks of noble individualities. Oh, I was learning! And the lessons were great! But then they had but just commenced.

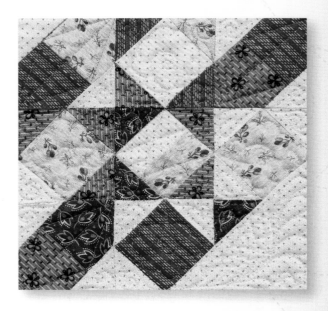

[85]

PATCHWORK BEDSPREAD

BLOCK SIZE:
8"
(20.3 CM)
SQUARE

A Neighbor's Idea

[53]

HOPES AND WISHES

BLOCK SIZE:
8"
(20.3 CM)
SQUARE

My faithful water boy, Hedrick, from a nearby homestead, at last had to give up the task of keeping my barrel filled—they had found something else for him to do in his spare time at home. I hoped in time to be able to toss the dice of chance for a well but was not yet in position to take so great a risk. They had a good well at Dave Heathlowe's and I thought that at least one of their two younger sons could be spared to haul water for me once in a week or perhaps two weeks. Mary Heathlowe had the same idea and before I had said a word about the matter suggested it to me—she was ready to take the whole world under her wing and she certainly did want me to make good. "Pa may object," she said, "he gets fussy sometimes but if he does, I'll fix it up. The boys like you and—you don't need to pay a cent. We can afford to do that much for a neighbor!"

However, I knew something about Dave Heathlowe's disposition and insisted that I would pay.

PART 5: KEEPING THE WATER BARREL FILLED

Spiritual Cactus

Six days of the week Dave Heathlowe farmed. On the seventh day, he put on a worn black suit, well blacked boots, carried a big Bible under his arm, rounded up his big family and went to town to preach in one of the two small box-like churches of Nesterville—neither one of which could in any sense support a preacher and neither one of which commanded anything like a proportionate membership out of the rapidly incoming army of homesteaders. But Dave Heathlowe was nothing if he was not aggressive and he drove souls before him as relentlessly as he drove his team over the unpaved trails, and his family over what he conceived to be the path of duty.

I had all my life been a regular churchgoer but I found myself not sorry that I was too far from town to gather frequently with the faithful under this man's ministrations. The ugly little meeting house, whose eight glaring windows remained hermetically sealed the year around and whose one door was the sole source of ventilation, had, however, a reason for being aside from the bitter gospel to which its undecorated walls reechoed. The preacher offered to our thirsty minds something that might well be compared to the alkali water of the plains and led our feet over spiritual cactus of the most painful type . . .

[68]

MEETING HOUSE SQUARE

BLOCK SIZE:
8"
(20.3 CM)
SQUARE

A Throne of Grace

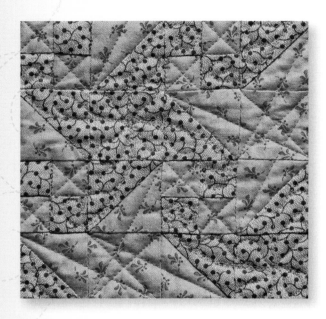

Bᵤt after he [Dave Heathlowe] had done his worst and the last awful attempt at song was come to an end, the pioneers had a real meeting "around a throne of grace"—the grace of natural, essential, kindly human fellowship. All strangers in a strange land, they were glad even for half an hour to exchange friendly handshakes, scraps of news, and enjoy together, perhaps not a "communion of saints" but a community of human feeling and fellowship which they needed fully as much as the hard ground needed rain from heaven.

[42]

FRIENDLY HAND

BLOCK SIZE:
6"
(15.2 CM)
SQUARE

No Help from Him

The Sunday following Mary's suggestion about water, I was able to attend service. It was a hot day and the little wooden box, filled with the odor of bodies more or less unwashed and of breath from lungs more or less unclean, and resounding to the harsh shouts of the preacher was not an inviting proposition, but one learns to bear.

After the service, which the preacher always drew out as lengthily as possible, having borne so far, I summoned all the latent grace in me and extended my hand to Dave Heathlowe to express as best I might some decent appreciation of his strenuous endeavors to set our feet in the right path. He eyed me coldly from his gaunt height and spoke first, loudly enough so that all in the room could hear.

"I understand you want us to haul water for you. Well, we can't do that. My boys' time belongs to me until they are of age. You'll have to look out for yourself. We had to when we came. You should have thought about these things before you came."

I saw gentle Mary stoop down to pick up a book, turning her face aside to wipe a sudden tear. I saw the preacher's youngest son, Harry, give his father a look such as bode no good for the young man's loyalty to that father in days to come. Quietly I answered the man that it was quite all right—I should be abundantly cared for without any help from him—and left the church. Nor should I ever have entered it again but for the fact that stronger than all other considerations was the fact that the little building, open once a week, did afford a gathering place for our socially starved selves.

[1]

A SUDDEN TEAR

BLOCK SIZE:
6"
(15.2 CM)
SQUARE

House of Unhewn Stone

[4]

BACHELOR'S PUZZLE

BLOCK SIZE:
8"
(20.3 CM)
SQUARE

My next and only known recourse—unless a second "raven" like unto Hedrick appeared—was a man whom I shall call A.Q., who owned the homestead next to mine. Thus far he had been something of a myth. His quarter section on which he had filed "sight unseen," had turned out to be absolutely no good except for rough pasture and not very good for that. He earned his sour-dough bread and flapjacks by cutting and hauling logs for the homesteaders from the distant timber, and spent a minority of his time on his claim. He kept some stock on the place and had a good well with a windmill and a trough. His tiny, one-roomed house of unhewn stone, so low and gray that it fairly melted into the general landscape, was only a mile from my cabin but the way was so rough that between lame feet and fear of loose cattle, the distance was practically prohibitive. A blank wall of his house turned toward Cabin O'Wildwinds so that I could not see his semi-occasional lamplight. Only the thin trail of smoke that semi-occasionally came from the low stovepipe that served him instead of a chimney reported his presence. His cattle barn, low-built of logs, lay still farther away and he used a gate leading to a road at the farthest point from Wildwinds. Up to this time I never had seen the man, but someone told me he was a "right decent little bachelor."

The Spirited Maneuver

Aside from the imperative water need I was really curious for another study of character! City life does not give one quite the sharply-defined opportunities of getting at the very core of people's selves as does life under such conditions as I was then experiencing. So, pondering, I set out on foot to see the man A. Q.

There was no break in the fence between our quarter sections. I could not climb nor could I crawl through the wires. Therefore I selected a spot with a minimum of cactus and apparently clear of snakes, cautiously lay down flat on my back as close to the bottom wire as I could, carefully rolled over and there I was unsnagged, on my neighbor's land, my eyes all agog for the horned brutes that often bunched near the division fence to gaze with greedy eyes at the unattainable grass on my side. The first time I executed this maneuver, I did not like it a bit. I was too city-minded! But all that nonsense was soon taken out of me. It was indeed well to have the artificiality of a too conventional life broken up. As I learned to adapt myself to circumstances and laugh at obstructions, inconveniences and deprivations, I was fitting myself to meet all of life in the future with better spirit.

I made for the ugly little stone hut, passing as I did so, at least an eighth of a mile of fence decorated with the owner's washing—a clean array of blankets, overalls, shirts, socks—all of them showing need for a woman's needle but all of them as decent as plenty of water could make them.

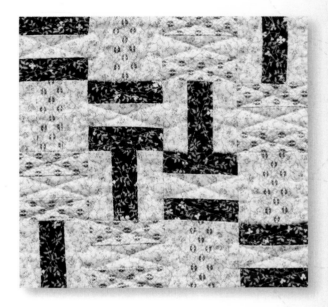

[38]

FENCE POSTS

BLOCK SIZE:
8"
(20.3 CM)
SQUARE

Decent Little Bachelor

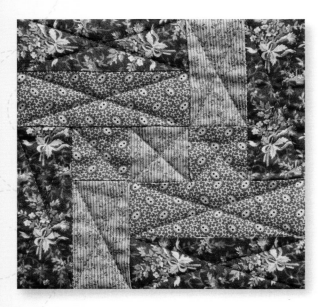

[109]

THAT WILD COUNTRY

BLOCK SIZE:
6"
(15.2 CM)
SQUARE

I "cried the house" and A. Q. came out to meet me, flushing scarlet up to the roots of his fair hair and with a frank honest gleam in his clear blue eyes—"a right decent little bachelor."

The wind is seldom still in that wild country and that morning it was blowing so hard that it snatched spoken words off our lips, making speech almost impossible, so my host invited me into his stone hut, gave me his one chair and seating himself on an upturned pail picked up three straws from the earth floor—through which there still protruded knobby vestiges of greasewood—and began industriously to braid them, wondering I suppose what in time "that there woman" was wanting. I explained. He was slow of speech but at least the argument began.

"Well—I ain't here always, you know. I've took up two claims—this here one and a desert claim away out yonder. When I ain't haulin' I'm liable to be at the other place. Couldn't Heathlowe's kids help you out? There's enough of them."

I further explained. The little man wagged his head and smiled. "Often the way with these here too-pious people," he offered. "That there kind of religion ain't no kind a-tall . . . But couldn't you make out to git what water you need at my pump yourself?

You're more'n welcome—ain't no bottom to the well—only thing on the place is worth anything. A woman alone like you be can't use such an all-fired lot of water?"

City Women on the Plains

I still further explained certain disabilities in the way of unable feet ankles and the daily need of my sixteen chickens, but he did not seem much impressed. I could see plainly that to him I was one of "these here" city women, a helpless breed he was not much acquainted with and perhaps did not have very much use for. However, he was gravely respectful.

"Of course, I could carry a little water at a time now and then," I said, in one final appeal, "but one must have water *always*. When it rains I put out pans under the eaves but one doesn't get much that way."

"No, this here country doesn't know how to rain!" he agreed grimly.

I was getting desperate. If this man refused me—"Heathlowe intimated that women alone like myself had no business on the plains, but I'm here and here I mean to stick and prove up—I have a RIGHT to. I may need a bit of help but—others may need my help some time. If they do, I'll give it if I can—up to the handle. If *I* had a well and horses and *you* needed water . . . and of course I expect to pay anything within reason."

[79]

NEED MY HELP

BLOCK SIZE:
8"
(20.3 CM)
SQUARE

Turkey Red Cotton

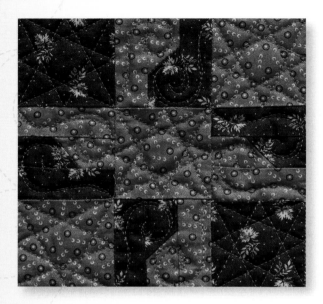

[40]

FLAG IN, FLAG OUT

BLOCK SIZE:
6"
(15.2 CM)
SQUARE

"We—ll . . ." He was now chewing his braided straws. I felt encouraged. "Matter of fact when I'm right busy you couldn't pay me what'd they *pay* me. See what I mean? How would seventy-five cents a barrel be? Time is all the money I've got. I can't promise to be regular nor often, but I'll do the best I can once I start in—that's my way. You hang a rag of some kind over your hitching post when you need me and when I'm home to see it I'll come over with a barrel full."

I walked back to Cabin O'Wildwinds almost on air—the wind blew so fiercely. The water problem taken care of was one long step toward success. I even forgot to watch for horned brutes. At once on reaching the house I got from my trunk a length of turkey red cotton which I happened to have and with a building slat, rigged up a signal flag and when the water in the barrel was more than two-thirds gone, tied it to the hitching post so that it hung high and flapped for my neighbor to see. Sometimes he happened to be at home and within a few hours his good horses with the stoneboat would be at the door. Sometimes it hung several days. Once it was out for two whole weeks with consequent anxiety and much inconvenience.

A. Q. kept to the letter of the bond but I had no reason to think that he ever hastened his return to his stone hut by a hoof's beat on my account. I also know that sometimes he could ill spare the time, but he never forgot or was careless.

More Than My Strength

During hot months I had to wrestle with shrinking staves and loosened hoops. It was a great game and full of unexpectedness. One day when I was away from the house, a wild gust of wind tore the back door screen loose, an investigating rooster got in and when I reached home I found him in the barrel, very much alive but very dejected. So was I. A. Q. was away for a long trip to the timber. At best, I could carry less than half a pailful at a time from his well and to make the trip twice in one day was more than my strength could meet. And when the horned brutes lay between me and the well nothing could have driven me on that side of the fence.

But the Lord does take care of children and fools, they say. During that particular period of enforced drought, no less than three different neighbors came to see me, none of them knowing my stress, but each of them bringing with them cans of water freshly drawn—they "kind o' thought" I'd like a drink of water less than two hours old.

[31]

DEJECTED ROOSTER

BLOCK SIZE:
8"
(20.3 CM)
SQUARE

The Outside Bathtub

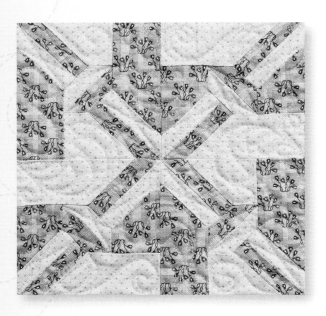

One lovely day when A. Q.'s cattle were grazing at the far side of the land, I had an inspiration. I nailed a stout rope to a grocery box, packed up in my tub, washboard, soap and soiled clothes, and with much toil dragged the load to the pump—a hard job for there was no beaten trail and the sod was rough with cattle holes and gnarly, thorny clumps of greasewood and cactus. But, breathless, I arrived. There was no hurry. I washed and washed and washed. Then I had another daring idea. How about a bath? I always carried my good field glasses with me and with them could scan the entire plains for miles—no one could steal upon me. I filled the tub with that clean cool water, even rigging up a board to conduct the stream from the pump away from the cattle trough to my tub. And I washed and I laved and I splashed as I had not washed and laved and splashed since leaving Chicago and bathtubs.

[57]

INSPIRATION PATCH

BLOCK SIZE:
8"
(20.3 CM)
SQUARE

My Ambition Ran Tall

I had filed on my quarter section under the description of hay-claim and could have satisfied the Government without further attempt at cultivation by proof that I had cropped the hay. But my ambition ran tall. I was filled and thrilled with the thought of soil redemption—the taming of the wilderness so that it should produce grain and support human life. So I meant, in addition to cropping the blue stem that covered my flat land, to see what could be done to cultivate the rough greasewood-and-cactus-covered rises, on one of which little Cabin O'Wildwinds was built.

While these first months of being fitted into the new life were moving by, my grass was growing splendidly for there had been an unusual snowfall and some good early rains. A civil engineer who had been on the plains for many years and understood soils and their cultivation down to the last syllable, told me—sketchily—as mere men so often give information to mere women—that my greasewood "rises" were "a proposition" agriculturally considered.

"Of course," he drawled, "cultivation can do something for this gumbo but it will take time. If you have money to spare to hire labor it will not do any harm to experiment."

[8]

BEGINNER'S DELIGHT

BLOCK SIZE:
6"
(15.2 CM)
SQUARE

All Mapped Out

[32]

DESERT GARDENING

BLOCK SIZE:
6"
(15.2 CM)
SQUARE

Experiment! I meant to have a vegetable garden, flowers, and, as a beginning, ten acres of oats. That was settled. I had bought seeds in the very earliest day of spring—I laugh now as I think of that ambitious, careful list which I mailed with a hard-to-spare check to a good florist in the state. And before the frost was out of the ground I had prevailed on A. Q., the only available man with horses and machinery, to promise to break an acre of ground for my garden near the house and ten acres for the oats. He shook his blond head and smiled. "Well, it's your funeral!" I thought he was a pessimist. I knew a little something about gardening and I meant to know more.

I had been reading everything I could find about the breaking up and cultivation of new ground and had my campaign all mapped out! Oats, that first year, ten acres of them; then winter wheat on that ten acres and an additional ten in oats; then alfalfa to follow the wheat, wheat to follow the oats, and ten more acres for oats—wheat—alfalfa. So before my homesteading term—which was five years when I filed, but was changed to three later on—was over, I would have a permanent stand of thirty acres of alfalfa and if I had two crops a year, that would be a big help. The father of a distant neighbor was an alfalfa enthusiast and I had learned even to make alfalfa tea—a brew that was supposed to be full of nourishment and vitality-essence; the word vitamin was not on the map then.

PART 6: GARDENING ON THE HOMESTEAD

Country of My Adoption

Very big I felt with all my acquired wisdom. But I had reckoned without experience and the first snag I struck was A. Q.'s mortal slowness in getting around to break the ten acres—one week he was too busy, another week the ground was too wet, another week he simply was not to be found, and at last it was admittedly too late to do anything that year. But he did get the one acre for garden broken up and perhaps I shall not be too greatly laughed at if I narrate that when he was all ready to turn the first furrow, I begged to have my hands on one of the plow handles and help the shining share cut the first sod on my own land. I can still see A. Q.'s superior, tolerant smile. Oh, but I was proud! All the latent love in me of Nature, of soil, of growing things, surged to the surface. And I was a true patriot and pioneer—helping to develop the beloved country of my adoption.

[78]

MY COUNTRY

BLOCK SIZE:
8"
(20.3 CM)
SQUARE

Not to Be Beaten

[95]

ROCKY MOUNTAIN

BLOCK SIZE:
6"
(15.2 CM)
SQUARE

I had studied Government bulletins about plowing. Ever since I can remember, the sight of a smoothly plowed field ready for the living seed has inspired a wonderful, almost a holy joy in me. So I waited eagerly to see my acre plowed. Ah me! I suppose A. Q. did his best but the rows of overturned sod that should have been even, level, the responsive soil, rippling along like waves, were anything else but! Every few feet, the plowshare, guided by A. Q.'s inadequate strength would leap clear of the ground refusing to do battle with the tough sod and snags of greasewood. Then again the bright steel would bite deeply and cast up a mound out of all proportion to the rest of the furrows. 'Twas a rough job. And although he had promised and I was willing and ready to pay, my little neighbor never did "get around" with his harrow—perhaps he saw it was no use and thought he would just let me find it all out for myself.

I was slow to convince. I did not propose to be beaten. I had bought a complete outfit of good garden tools, so with new spade, new hoe, new rake, new spud, new trowel, new stakes for string and new string for the new stakes, I set out to have a garden and grow food for the coming winter. The Great Mother seemed to smile on me: The Rocky Mountains loomed above the horizon in marvelous peaks and shoulders of shining, snow-crowned beauty; the birds—meadow larks, curlews, tiny song birds whose names I did not know—filled the air with joy; the tonic air was as wine; the enterprise on which I had embarked was thrilling—sacred even. . . .

Just Lie Fallowing

I struck my shining hoe into the soil. I forbear to write the complete story of my defeat. Enough to say that after three days of futile struggle I staked out a scrap of ground about the size of a kitchen table and by dint of sweat of brow and ache of back, thrashed it into an appearance of smoothness and planted a few handy seeds—lettuce, radishes, onions. Beside my little porch I buried hopefully some morning-glory and scarlet bean seeds, in memory of a vine-covered summerhouse that had been the joy of my early childhood.

Somewhere in my reading a word had caught my imagination and I now comforted myself with it. Fallow. When ground that had been ploughed lay fallow, I understood, the fingers of the light and the rain did a work all their own upon stubborn soil until it was rendered friable—willing to support green life. Perhaps it was just as well that A. Q. had not bothered to harrow the acre— it should just lie fallowing for a twelvemonth. Lie fallowing. The words tasted good in my mouth and consoled me as day by day and week by week I watched my kitchen-table plot. Not a thing sprouted. There was almost no rain. The sun was scorching hot. The gumbo was unkind. One morning-glory seed sent up a pale leaf which died. I swallowed and then smiled, surveying my grass land. No failure there!

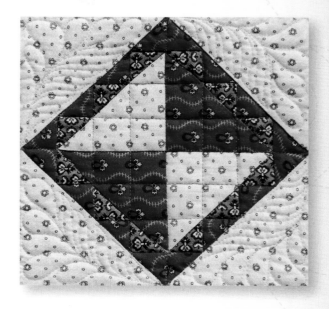

[115]

VINES AT THE WINDOW

BLOCK SIZE:
8"
(20.3 CM)
SQUARE

The Ripe Hay

Then the hay was ripe. The skies had been kind. The grass was tall and thick. And who should apply for permission to cut and stack it on shares but Dave Heathlowe who had been so unkind? As he had a mowing machine and as there was no other man I could hire or bribe, the job went to him. I rather hated—sentimentally—to see those lovely acres of rippling life laid low, but cash is cash and another spring would re-dress the field. Heathlowe did not deserve the privilege, but as I have reported his hardness so I must record his faithfulness—he turned out to be prompt, honest, thorough-going in every detail of the work, wasted no hay, took no more than his share, found me a good customer, exacted cash and turned it over on the hour—honest as he was hard.

[77]

MOWING MACHINE QUILT

BLOCK SIZE:
6"
(15.2 CM)
SQUARE

PART 6: GARDENING ON THE HOMESTEAD

Seems All Right

With the hay money safely banked I decided to take a flyer in water. A. Q. had two brothers who were well drillers. I sent word to them to come and talk well. They were entirely frank: hiring a well drilled was "the gamblingest kind of a gamble" they said. They "hated to see a widder woman lose out." But then I might win. One of the brothers had drilled thirteen times on his claim and had not even moistened his drill. If water came it might be bad.

Well," I said, boldly, "nothing venture, nothing have! If I am to stay on this place and turn it into anything like a farm I've got to have plenty of water. When can you start drilling?"

On the afternoon of the third day a shout: *Water!* The men sampled muddy mouthfuls and spat discriminatingly. "Seems all right," they said. They drew a bucketful and set it inside the cabin to settle till morning when they would return. If after tasting it thoroughly I decided it was right, they would drill a few feet farther to make it a real well, then put down galvanized iron casing, set up a pump and congratulate me.

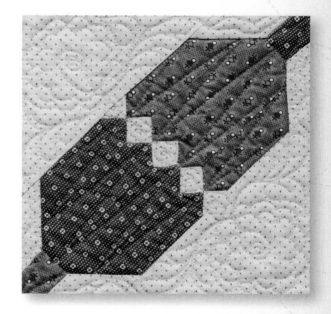

[16]

BROTHERS

BLOCK SIZE:
8"
(20.3 CM)
SQUARE

Unutterable Woe

[20]

CELEBRATION

BLOCK SIZE:
6"
(15.2 CM)
SQUARE

I awoke at dawn, tasted gingerly, sipped, drank a little, drank more, lifted my heart up to heaven in thankfulness. It surely was perfectly sweet water. "Struck lie?" shouted the men as they rode up to the house, two on one horse, and threw up their hats when I told them. They did the extra drilling. What a dinner I cooked that day! A huge pan of biscuits standing up on crisp brown full three inches; broad thick slices of pink-and-white bacon—no curled slivers for western appetites; plenty of canned tomatoes; a mound of rice; I even rashly opened a can of salmon; made all the coffee, clear and strong, we could possibly consume—no need now to watch the barrel; and went so far as to set a pitcher filled with water on the table—the last of the barrel stuff I should have to use, for by night the pump would be installed and in the morning I should draw heaven's free gift out of the bosom of the earth.

In the morning I pumped.

Woe, woe, unutterable woe. The Great Mother had dealt me the hardest slap yet. For the water that gushed easily out of the pump mouth was salt, bitter, acrid—I could not hold it in my mouth.

Blaming Themselves

News of the "widder's" good luck had spread and before noon several teams were lined up before the house. A good well means a lot to a growing community. A. Q.'s well had helped to locate me. Mine would help to locate others. The drillers came— heard—swore. I begged them to go right on swearing. They even blamed themselves a little for they thought that in drilling the few extra feet to make it "a real well," as they expressed it, they had tapped a lower, freer stream flowing out of hell's washpot.

After the first bitter hour—as bitter as the water itself—I shrugged my shoulders, set my teeth, took a long look at the shining shoulders of the distant mountains, fastened my flag in place and thanked God for a neighbor and a barrel. I mailed the drillers their checks, got out my dictionary and typewriter and went to work to try to earn the money I must have if the dog and cat were to be fed and Mary's chickens thrive.

[10]

BITTER WASHPOT

BLOCK SIZE:
6"
(15.2 CM)
SQUARE

Pure as a Royal Diamond

[118]

WATER RICH

BLOCK SIZE:
6"
(15.2 CM)
SQUARE

Two years later a man offered to dig me a well by hand for a very moderate sum of money and I bade him go ahead. He struck water not very deep down. It was not any too sweet but it served and when cold was quite swallowable. True, it turned tea black and made coffee bitter but it was wet and harmless and plentiful. By that time I was thoroughly *"water-broke"* and grumbled no more. But I did not entirely abandon the blessed barrel. When winter came I melted enough snow to fill to the brim and let it freeze. Then when I wanted a truly marvelous drink I hacked out chunks of ice and melted them. That was water! Absolutely pure and as limpid as a royal diamond.

It so happened that while I was writing these paragraphs, the thermometer stood at nearly 100 degrees. The iceman had failed to come. The faucet water is warm and unpleasant, for now so artificial have we become that we are forced to "treat" city water with chemicals to make it soft and safe. I was on the point of grumbling when I had a vision—a distant mountain shoulder, a tiny kitchen with a barrel in the corner—I smiled and drank the city water smiling, nor had I any harsh judgment for the wail of a fellow woman, who never having been water poor does not know when she is water rich.

Two Frequent Questions

Of the hundreds of questions asked me by people curious to know the experiences of an elderly city woman "holding down" a homestead all sole alone on the Great Plains, two have been put more frequently than others and always accompanied with a tone of consternation or a note of actual horror: "Did you not get fearfully lonely?" "And weren't you AFRAID?"

Briefly—yes, to both questions, a big, emphatic yes. But there is more to tell than this mere admission. *How* I lived through the loneliness and *how* I finally conquered fear, are a vital part of these simple annals which contain nothing of mystery, little of romance, no heroics, but a great deal of genuine human struggle.

[56]

INDEPENDENCE SQUARE

BLOCK SIZE:
8"
(20.3 CM)
SQUARE

My Sole Companions

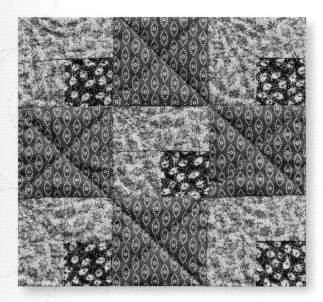

[89]

PUSS IN THE CORNER

BLOCK SIZE:
6"
(15.2 CM)
SQUARE

In chapters preceding this one I have used the word neighbors more than once and may have given the impression of more companionship than I really had or could have. My nearest neighbor was A. Q., whom I saw for a few minutes when he brought water or when he came to work for me, and as he had but little time to spare and was away from his homestead a major part of the time, his calls were brief, few and far between. After I had a well and after I abandoned the struggle with the soil, I practically saw nothing more of him.

Further away than A. Q. were the Heathlowes. Mary was able to visit me perhaps once in two months and not so often in winter. I went to her home only when I was forced to, for the walk was long and fearfully rough with fences between.

Day after day after day, Lassie and Betsy Bobbett, dog and cat, were my sole companions. The sixteen incubator chickens Mary had forced upon me were nothing but a nuisance, a care and an expense. I thought of investing in a horse and conveyance but if I had done that I should have had to do fencing, build the animal a shelter and furnish it with water and feed, and these things I could not do.

There was a horse dealer, Tom Elliott, whose quarter section and big log house of one room was a good distance from Wildwinds. He and his band of shouting, wild-riding men often passed my place and occasionally took a short-cut through, though they never stopped at the house or in any way troubled me. One day, while out driving with a neighbor, we stopped at his empty cabin to take shelter from a sudden hailstorm. The inside of that cabin did not predispose my mind comfortably toward its owner and his men, for certain "city notions" still clung to me.

The "furniture" consisted of a huge table of rough planks, broken chairs and battered stools, bunks—three-tiered—along one side wall, an immense kitchen range, rusty, greasy and overflowing with ashes. Dirty dishes, discarded clothing, empty tin cans, cigarette stubs, burned matches, tools, quirts, odds and ends of saddle equipment, evidences of mice and cockroaches—it was not a pretty sight and the complement of empty whisky flasks did not help matters any. But, until this winter night of which I have to tell, I never saw Elliott at close range and then—but hear the little tale.

Lassie's Low Growl

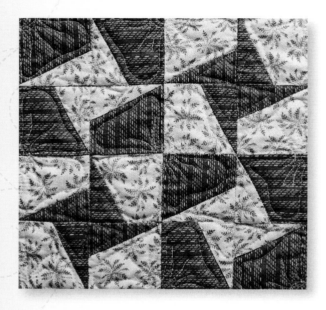

It was bitterly cold. As a matter of conservation of warmth, Lassie was sleeping on her own blanket on my bed. I had no way of keeping a fire all night so when I read myself to sleep as I nearly always did—to keep my thoughts from running wild—I put on a wool cap and had thick mittens on my hands. That night it was thirty-five below by the thermometer on the porch and very little less in the house. It was after midnight, for one of my spells of being afraid was on me and sleep would not come. Suddenly, Lassie lifted her head and pricked her ears. She could hear sounds long before I could though my own hearing was too keen for comfort. A low growl began far down in her throat. I laid my hand on her muzzle, a sign for silence which she perfectly understood and always obeyed. The hair rose stiffly along her spine—she did not like what she heard. Then it came to me; the swift trotting of a horse and a man's voice—swearing. Fairly nauseated with fear I instantly blew out the light.

[121]

WINTER'S NIGHT

BLOCK SIZE:
8"
(20.3 CM)
SQUARE

What's Wanted?

Then through the thin door came a shout: "Hello! Hello! Hello! Anyone to home?" Of course he had seen the light. If he had not, he might force the door in—he might do that anyway. I lay rigid, breath held, Lassie quivering to be up and at the door. "Hello! Hello! This is Elliott—Tom Elliott!" The door handle was vigorously rattled, then came a good push. At that I released Lassie who sprang barking to the door, threw back the bed cloths and scrambled out, calling what I tried to make a natural voice, "Yes, Mr. Elliott! What's wanted?" I thought my last hour was come.

Instantly the voice changed and in respectful, even musical tones, my midnight caller made his wishes known. "Awful sorry to bother you, ma'am. But could you let me have some kerosene an' matches? When we left my place there was none and I clean forgot to get any and none of the boys will be in. I been a long ride after some horses and I ain't had a bite to eat since noon. I used my last match just now! I got a bottle here if you could let me have some kerosene."

"Yes, indeed!" I answered and with shaking hands lighted my lamp and unlocked the door. "I haven't any fire," I chattered, putting out my hand to take the bottle he thrust toward me.

"That's all right, ma'am! I wasn't aimin' to come in this time o' night—'most mornin' ain't it?" I could feel his broad smile as he pulled the door shut on himself.

[71]

MIDNIGHT CALLER

BLOCK SIZE:
8"
(20.3 CM)
SQUARE

Courtesy on the Plains

[105]

SUNSHINY DAY

BLOCK SIZE:
8"
(20.3 CM)
SQUARE

I filled the bottle and took a full box of matches from my supply. If it had been daytime I should have offered him at least hot coffee—the unfailing beverage of courtesy on the plains. I thrust the bottle and matches through the partly opened door, he took them, thanked me heartily and rode off, swearing steadily at his horse. As he turned away the wind flung in my face a full blast of liquor from his breath.

No sleep for me that night! I lighted a good fire, made coffee for myself, dressed, and sat down to write letters till morning.

Two days later a genial chinook was blowing, the sun shining, and at noon I was sitting out on my porch enjoying the ever-changing panorama of the mountains, when a horseman appeared, Tom Elliott, in full plains regalia from spurs to chaps, gay neckerchief, broad sombrero, quirt, guns, lariat. He was mounted on a magnificent horse and as he drew close to the house he set it to prancing and dancing and whirling—boyishly showing off for my benefit. Tied to his saddle horn was a bottle of kerosene which he presented to me with an elaborate bow and smile, and in answer to my invitation to "light," joined me on the porch.

A Real Western Man

"You sure was scared when I come the other night, ma'am. I sure was sorry," he apologized gravely. "I'd ought to have gone somewheres else. But if you was a real western born woman," he continued, regarding me out of keen, kindly, blue eyes, "you'd have knew better than to be scared! Me, I'm born to this here country. I hate cities like pizen. I'd die in Chicago or New York. Been on horseback since I could walk—before that, mebbe! An' I'm here to tell you a real western man has to be a heap rottener than I've ever saw them to bother a woman who don't want to be bothered . . ."

[21]

CHICAGO STAR

BLOCK SIZE:
8"
(20.3 CM)
SQUARE

Here Is God's Country

[35]

FAR WEST

BLOCK SIZE:
8"
(20.3 CM)
SQUARE

" . . . Oh, sometimes they get drunk on rotten whiskey and forget theirselves, but 'tain't offen and a good woman could bring 'em to their senses soon enough. Don't you never be scared no more, ma'am. You don't even need to lock your door—you're a heap safer here, I take it, than you ever was in the city you come from. This here is God's country!" and he [Tom Elliott] gazed off at the glistening mountain ranges and something came into his eyes that was very like reverence and worship. "Well, I'll mosey. Thanks awfully for the oil an' matches. An' if there's ever anything I can do for you just say the word! So long!"

Rearing, whirling, fancy-stepping his horse carried him out of sight—a real western man and a friend, should I need him.

But not yet was I cured of fear, the unreasoning, causeless fear that tensed nerves and hurried heartbeats when night came on. The foolish things I did are too foolish to tell about. On moonless, starless nights, when impenetrable darkness surrounded the cabin, I used to peer out of the door and tremble at the immensity through which I could not see. Mother Nature had no attraction for me then. Although my reason and intelligence told me that the plains were the same at night as they were in the daytime, the fear side of me peopled them with prowling dangers and I simply could not bear it!

A Curtain Drew Aside

If this went on, I should be a wreck—it had to be stopped. Easier said than done! Came a fearful night when I went to the bottom of panic—for no specific cause at all save that I knew a determined child could have broken in and that I was far from any human help no matter what happened. It was an absolutely dark night, with the wind blowing "great guns." My reasoning self knew that there would be no riders out save those who had business to be. And the animal life of the plains was nothing to be dreaded. I was just plain afraid. All at once shame seized me. I sat up in bed with clenched fists. If there had been any possible way of escaping back to what then seemed to me to be "God's country,"—the city of noises and crowding people and street lights and telephones and policemen, I should have taken it with one flying leap. But the little Cabin and the impenetrable darkness held me. Then— apropos of nothing except my need—a verse of Scripture rang in my memory clear as a spoken voice: "The angel of the Lord encampeth round about them that fear Him and delivereth them." *Fear Him!* A curtain drew aside in my thought and for an instant I had a vision—a picture of a fearless world, a world wherein there was nothing to injure or make afraid, a world perfectly obedient to the perfect law and will of One—such a world as there has not been since Paradise, so the record goes.

[84]

OUT OF THIS WORLD

BLOCK SIZE:
6"
(15.2 CM)
SQUARE

Whispered the Lord's Prayer

[58]

KEPT FROM HARM

BLOCK SIZE:
8"
(20.3 CM)
SQUARE

Then I began to think more coherently, reasoning with myself: I was where I was by reason of a choice made as the best thing I could do at the time I did it—I had ill will to none—I was doing my best each day to live sanely and constructively—why should I be afraid of anything or anyone, particularly why should I be afraid without known cause? I did not have the blind faith that could "see" as with inner vision any bright visitant from another world making encampment round and about my lowly Cabin but I thought it was entirely possible that when one was doing one's truly best, one would be cared for and kept from evil. Indeed, that is the heart and core of the Christian's belief, and so far as in me lay I was a Christian. I whispered the Lord's prayer in the darkness, and after it the little invocation of babyhood, "Now I lay me down to sleep," snuggled down on my pillow and from that hour to this, fear of that kind has never troubled me.

There still remained specific victories I had to win over other forms of timidity and unwontedness, but while I stayed on the plains and since leaving them, even until now, baseless, foolish, craven fear has not dared to lift its head. Perhaps on some great day—in another world if not in this—even as the prophet's eyes were opened so that he saw the surrounding armies of the Lord, so I shall see and understand how relief from the intolerable situation could come about. For I know that there are better women than I who never get away from fear in its many forms. Perhaps they do not try!

PART 8: OVERCOMING FEARFULNESS

First Winter's Snowfall

Just as there came that night when I sank to the depths of fear, so there came a day when I drained the cup of solitude to its dregs. It was during my first winter in Cabin O'Wildwinds. Following a snowfall that had turned the great expanse of the plains to a blinding unrelieved white, there were ten days of such intense cold that only those ventured out who were forced to go. Faces froze in the dry still air before their owners knew what was happening to them. From my windows all I could see was blazing empty stillness with the silent mountains on the horizon and at night the silent wheel of the pitiless stars.

[102]

STAR OVER THE MOUNTAIN

BLOCK SIZE:
6"
(15.2 CM)
SQUARE

Keeping Warm and Alive

Not a cloud in the sky, not a shadow on the ground, not a sound in the world save the creak and snap of the wee house's timbers. In all that time I was alone with one thing to do—keep warm and alive and as busy as my inventiveness could keep me. I sewed, wrote, read, cleaned a perfectly clean little house, tidied perfectly tidy shelves, broke up a packing case and made myself an extra table, answered all my letters at quite unnecessary length and stamped them ready for mailing only heaven knew when, visited the chickens in their horrid little shed expecting to find them frozen every time I did so, experimented in cooking new dishes out of the same old canned goods, and then did everything over again—spending much time peering out of my window until vision went black from the glare.

[88]

POSTAGE STAMP

BLOCK SIZE:
6"
(15.2 CM)
SQUARE

A Vegetable Soup Party

And the second Sunday—Sundays always seemed more lonely—was the tenth day. I awoke at dawn possessed by a nervous energy that could have accomplished almost anything but there just was nothing to do. Childishly, at noon, the sun still unclouded, the trails still empty, the cold still unbroken, the wind still asleep, I decided to have a party. What I was really doing was trying to keep my nerve, tensed almost to the breaking point. So I got out my best tablecloth and napkin, set the new table I had made with my prettiest possessions, cooked an elaborate creamed vegetable soup which took a long time to make, having to be run through a colander, put on my one party dress, even stuck a velvet rose in my hair, and bidding Lassie and Betsy Bobbett, my perfectly serene and comfortable dog and cat, sit on two chairs near the table, proceeded to dish up. I filled a valuable blue plate with the savory hot soup and on the way from kitchen to table, stumbled, the soup burned my hand, and—with a scream which I never knew was in me, hurled the full plate across the room and running to my bed, burst into convulsive crying. The little scald on my hand was nothing. The explosion was in my mind.

[14]

BROKEN DISHES

BLOCK SIZE:
6"
(15.2 CM)
SQUARE

That's Perfectly All-Right!

[66]

LONELINESS

BLOCK SIZE:
8"
(20.3 CM)
SQUARE

In the midst of the storm I realized perfectly something had to be done—I had to see someone or go somewhere, no matter what the danger of freezing on the way. I would see if possibly A. Q. was at home and either go to him or get him to come to me. Yes, smoke was coming out of the stovepipe, the smoke of a freshly built fire. I took my big dishpan and a huge iron spoon, and standing on my back porch made such a clatter as that peaceful world had never before heard. In a few minutes the little man was out beside his house to see what it was all about, waved an arm to me and I knew he would come over. Presently he did and as I opened the door and his three dogs pushed into the warmth of the house, I grabbed his sleeve and almost crying again, cried, "A. Q.! If you don't come in here and talk to me I shall go crazy! I haven't seen a soul—"

He gave me a keen comprehensive glance and saying, as if to reassure me, "That's perfectly all-right!" came in, divested himself of several mufflers and coats and sat down beside the stove, asking no questions until I of myself had confessed to the tale of my nervousness and the broken soup plate.

Discussing Every Topic

"If you had not been home," I said, but he did not let me complete the sentence, but lifting an admonitary hand assured me once again, "That's perfectly all-right! Good gosh! I don't blame you none. If I didn't have my horses and work that takes me into town every so often, I'd be the same. I get goofy sometimes up in the timber—or I would if I didn't have to get the logs out and keep goin'. I don't rightly see how you stand it here—it's no place for a woman alone. Now some of these here *girls* who stake out claims, they just naturally draw folks—the young fellers see to that. But with an older woman it's different. . . . Right smart cold, isn't it?" and therewith we began to talk on any and every topic. It never occurred to me to ask my enforced caller if he had had his dinner. We discussed homesteading, homesteaders, politics, religion, crops—the great crop I was going to have the coming autumn. The four dogs and the cat stretched and snored by the fire. The wood fairly melted in the stove. The shadow of the house on the snow steadily shifted. It drew on toward dusk. Then I made coffee and set out a lunch—a mere snack. I rather loathed food just then. As I poured my guest a third cup of coffee, somehow he brought out that this was his first meal that day. He had come in late the night before almost frozen stiff. Had put two stone jugs of boiling hot water in his bunk and getting "good and warm" had not ventured forth until not long before he heard my rataplan calling him. He had cared for his horses but had not had time to care for himself.

"And you've had nothing to eat since some time yesterday?" I cried, ashamed of my selfishness. "Can you stand it a little longer?"

[114]

UP ALL NIGHT

BLOCK SIZE:
6"
(15.2 CM)
SQUARE

The Big Ben Clock

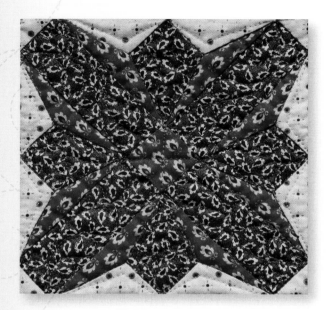

[55]

IDLE HOURS

BLOCK SIZE:
6"
(15.2 CM)
SQUARE

So then I got out the best I had and cooked a real meal and had my reward in seeing the man eat and in my own renewed appetite. The meal over, we renewed our fireside conversation—books, farming, crops for new homestead—alfalfa, oats, rye, flax, corn, wheat, logging, homesteading in all its aspects, politics, religion. The dogs were let out and let in. The brilliant light of the full moon on the floor made the lamplight look sickly. I began to feel tired. A. Q. began to yawn. The animals were dead in sleep. Then—

"I wonder what time does it say by that there clock o' yourn? Is it right?" suggested my guest, flushing to the roots of his hair. My Big Ben was on the shelf above my head—I had not glanced at it since cooking the late dinner. I took it down, listened—it was running steadily—held it out to A. Q. He roared with laughter and uttered a smothered "Good Gosh!" It was Monday morning and more. We had talked twelve hours straight and it is safely to be conjectured that in all his sober, conscientious, well-moderated life, little New England A. Q., bachelor, never before had been guilty of visiting the clock around alone with a woman!

The humor of the situation overcame us both, and our laughter was good for my nerves. I accompanied my guest outside to see what the thermometer had to say. Forty-six below in the moonlight and still dropping. I speeded the parting guest, who stood to give me a backward glance and say humorously, "I'm thinking it's a mighty good thing we've got no neighbors. They *might* talk!" and our mutual laughter again rang out in the frozen world.

Refreshed as a Child

When I awoke toward noon of the next day, as refreshed as a child from a happy sleep, the entire face of the plains was changed. Shadows drifted across the snow, wind and mercury were rising, there were teams and riders on the trails, and before the afternoon was gone, friends at the door. But I told no one of the episode just narrated—it would do no good and would only add to my neighbors' anxiety about me and they had enough of their own.

Very little effect has solitude had upon me since. I learned in those years on the plains how to do without the physical presence of people. But, what was of even greater value—I also learned to value the human unit as never before.

[62]

LIGHT AND SHADOWS

BLOCK SIZE:
6"
(15.2 CM)
SQUARE

The Dark of the Moon

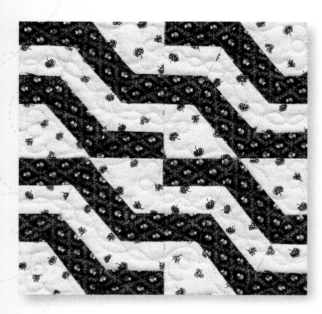

[119]

WINDING TRAIL

BLOCK SIZE:
8"
(20.3 CM)
SQUARE

Psychologists tell us we are afraid of that which we do not understand—the unknown. There was one vast unknown I greatly wished to explore but it took some time before I could command myself sufficiently to go forward. After the sun was gone down I found it more than difficult to stay out-of-doors in the darkness. On moonlit nights I sat on my little porch—my back close against the wall of the house—and drank in the wonder of the scene—the distant mountains veiled in snow, stars whose brilliance were not overcome by the moonlight, and the stretching of the level plains, away and away and away to the horizon. But in the dark of the moon, I could not sit out for long, and I simply could not get any distance from the house, even with my flashlight. There "was something about it," as we say for want of a more intelligent phrase, that "got" me. I was familiar with every foot of my quarter section and the adjoining acres were the same as mine. I knew the roads and trails. I knew who lived in the widely-scattered shacks that winked their evening eyes at me; there was no wild life to fear—coyotes are cowards and they were the chiefest of the untamed things that still survived the coming of man. I would watch the sun go down—and the magnificence of those sunsets are beyond any power of mine to describe, would watch gentle night slowly slip into the room of day and know beyond a peradventure that the face of the plains was unchanged save for the venturing forth of small and harmless beasties that would flee before my slightest move. But for all this I could not stay out-of-doors for more than a brief sojourn—and would cravenly seek the comfort and stay of lamplight and enclosing walls.

The Well Platform

I had had a solid platform built around my pump, which was in front of the house and perhaps one hundred feet away. I installed on this platform a comfortable chair and a sizeable wooden box. Then when weather—and wind—permitted, I would light my good lantern, take it to the platform, smother its light in the box and seat myself, back to the house, face to the mountains. And there I tried to sit. It really was ridiculous. I was indeed a finished product of that artificial life and habit which robs man of the natural equipment with which he comes into the world—the occult sense by which he could feel at home anywhere and at any hour in the presence of Nature.

[12]

BOX

BLOCK SIZE:
6"
(15.2 CM)
SQUARE

The Great Book of Nature

[27]

CONSTELLATION

BLOCK SIZE:
8"
(20.3 CM)
SQUARE

My self-imposed schooling was at first not easy and all my attention was taken up with the will to stay. But little by little I lengthened my sittings, forcing myself to think on themes more or less connected with my marvellous environment. Thank the good Maker of us all for the law of Habit. By it man can overcome almost any handicap. In time I formed the habit of being out alone under the sunless sky and little by little the leaves of the great book of nature began to turn before my wondering watch. The vast procession of the constellations with here and there the brilliant—and relatively slow—passage of a meteor. The whisper of the wind as its wings brushed the earth or its great song as it swept far above on errands to the uttermost ends of the world. The call of some wild creature to its mate. Sleepy chirps of birds hiding in the grass, or nesting in the low greasewood and under the protection of the cactus thorns. Then that marvellous experience of *listening to the silence,* the inner self calm, new thoughts floating into consciousness from one's deeper depths, perhaps to be recalled by the weird cry of a coyote, distant or not so distant, with the keen realization that this little wild brother also had his right place in the scheme of things.

I Learned to Love

These things cannot be communicated by "cunning juxtaposition of words." Perhaps the term love will best serve my purpose: I learned through revealment to love the immensity of the night, the unfathomableness of sky, wind, stars, moon, mountains, silence, solitude, and that ineffable Something for which earth's vocabulary has no fit name, something realer than reality, "closer than hands and feet," Something which refreshes and cleanses from without to within so body, mind, and soul "feel better" for whatever is to come.

But I was not always to be thus alone—there was companionship on its way to me and when it came it was to be all the sweeter and dearer and more truly sacred because of what had gone before.

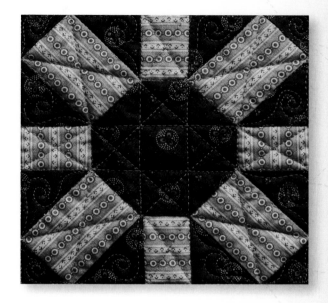

[72]

MIDSUMMER NIGHT

BLOCK SIZE:
6"
(15.2 CM)
SQUARE

Right Nice Folks

[17]

BUILDER'S BLOCK QUILT

BLOCK SIZE:
6"
(15.2 CM)
SQUARE

One morning while eating breakfast my ears were greeted with an unmistakable sound, the odd muffled sound of a plank dropped directly on other planks.

Planks? I stood up from the table, ears intent. Yes, planks, one after the other. I rushed out-of-doors, looked in every direction, and there to the southeast on the quarter section cornering mine was a lumber wagon and a man unloading planks. That meant building, building meant builders—people—a new shack perhaps? Forgetting the hot coffee, I covered the distance between myself and the wagon as speedily as possible praying it would not get away before I could have speech with the men. They had just dropped the last plank into place and the driver had the lines in his hands, but I called to them to wait a minute, which they did, and breathlessly I plied them with questions. The answers were brief and to the point.

"Yup! Yes'm. Guess he filed on it some time ago. House—not what you'd rightly call a shack. Barn, too, by the stuff he's bought. Yup! Man and fambly. He'll be along hisself tomorrow—he's goin' to do most of the work hisself—help's hard to get. Right nice folks I hearn tell. That your place yonder? Cute little house all right. How d'y'like it all by yourself? Lots o' greasewood hereabouts, ain't they? Snakes, too? Me, I've got sagebrush land. Yup. Two kids. Yup. Well, so long, lady!"

Good Farmer and Friend

I almost danced back to the Cabin. "Neighbors!" I shouted to Lassie who leaping up tried to lick my face, feeling the lift in my spirits and responding, loyal understanding little comrade that she always was. "Neighbors! Right nice folks. Two kids! A woman!"

Next morning early I was on watch, saw a wagon drive up and made for it, introducing myself to "hisself," the Optimist, as I later named him, the good farmer and friend who was to sow my land with golden grain—start me out on the high emprise of helping to furnish "bread for the world." He too answered my questions briefly but cordially. The little family had been bunking in an abandoned shack at a railroad station twelve miles down the line, where the trains stopped only on signal, waiting for their household stuff to come by slow freight. He had been afraid "the woman" and kids would be sick before he could get them under a roof of their own with a chance to do some decent cooking. He was going to get the house up just as fast as hard work would let him. If he could only hire two or three capable men to stay with it till the work was done but then they had come expecting hard conditions so must just do the best they could—he was sure if they did that, everything would be all right. He would tell "her" she had a neighbor already and I must come over just as soon as they moved in. I liked this newcomer!

[96]

SAGE BUD

BLOCK SIZE:
8"
(20.3 CM)
SQUARE

Light Piercing the Gloom

[50]

HAYES CORNER*

BLOCK SIZE:
6"
(15.2 CM)
SQUARE

Day by day boards clattered, saws sang, hammers beat out the blessed music of house building, home making, folks coming. And then one night, one dark, dark night following a day of misty rain when I had not been able to make out even with my glass just what was going on around the new house, a light suddenly pierced the gloom—the light of a kerosene lamp.

I whispered to myself, a rush of hot glad tears turning the lowly earth star into a burst of rays that glowed like a tiny sun. The newcomer's light had crossed the gulf of isolation for me—the only neighbor light to brighten the darkness since I had come to Cabin O'Wildwinds, save that first light I had seen beneath the rainbow arch and which, strangely, I never had seen again.

It was well there was no one to witness my feeling when I first saw that low-shining beam a mile away behind which an unknown sister woman spread their evening meal and hushed her little ones to rest.

*The family's last name was Hays.

A Gold-Letter Day

The light burned late—I yearned to go over to see if I could help in the settling. The next morning was Sunday. Indeed, Sundays were special days with me—not always red-letter days, it is true. But this was to be a gold-letter day. The sky was still stormy but nothing could have kept me away from the new house. I tried to wait a decent time after I saw the first smoke ascend from the chimney, then I was off.

The Optimist had been prompt and thorough with his fence building and as the road was at the far side of his quarter, no gate as yet connected his fence corner with mine. Their house was near the fence, however, and as I searched for a cactusless depression in the ground on which I might flatten myself out to roll under the barbed wire, I heard a child's sweet voice pipe up, "Papa! There's a lady out there—is she coming here?" Then, a little boy of about six came running out shouting eagerly, "My Mamma she says for you to come right on in— she's bathing the baby and can't come to the door!"

[22]

CHIMNEY

BLOCK SIZE:
6"
(15.2 CM)
SQUARE

A Home in the Making

[52]

HOMESPUN BLOCK

BLOCK SIZE:
8"
(20.3 CM)
SQUARE

Beside her kitchen range I found her, sweet Lizzie, the Optimist's wife, her naked babe laughing on her lap, not a girl wife but a mature woman to whom love and motherhood had come in her maturer years. At once we embraced like long separated friends. The little boy clutched my skirts and bubbled over with glee. The babe kicked and chuckled. The Optimist stood about and beamed upon us, an unfinished cup of coffee in his hand, his hat on his head.

"Take off your things—help her, Papa. Do make yourself at home! Isn't it good to have a neighbor come right at once! You won't mind the mess, will you?—we only got in last night."

Mess? What I saw was a lovely confusion of home-in-the-making: lumber and tools, furniture crated and uncrated, trunks and boxes, a pail of fresh milk, firewood dumped on the new floor, little clothes drying on strings stretched across a corner, the remains of a picnic breakfast on half a table, the other half piled with just unpacked dishes. Not a mess!— the possibility of a home.

I sat down beside the stove, the children were given some toys, and the man of the house went off to the barn. Lizzie's tongue and mine kept steady pace with the old Seth Thomas clock perched on top of a barrel until there could be a shelf built for it. And in what seemed to be no time at all it was noon.

You're Not Going?

"Why, of course, you'll stay to dinner! We can't let you go so soon! Don't know what there is to eat but there'll be something—this place seems like heaven to me after that awful shack down by the tracks."

I stayed. I forgot what we had to eat—ah, no, I *remember*! Nectar and ambrosia with a bacon rind for Lassie. . . . Hours later, tongues and the clock still were keeping pace, with the Optimist smoking peacefully nearby, dropping off now and then into a doze for he was a tired man and was in his own home for the first Sunday after many weary weeks. Then as the clouds had broken away and the level rays of the setting sun came through the unshaded windows, I looked about for my hat.

"You're not *going*? But why? Oh, you must stay for supper! I'll stir up some pancakes. Can you drink milk—like it? We have a real good cow. And I have three eggs left from some I bought from a woman we passed on the road—she let me have part of hers she had just got in town."

It was something more than pancakes and milk that was shared with me that evening—angels' food and wine of fellowship, with a bowl of morning's milk and scraps for Lassie. Then we sociably "did" the dishes, strained the milk and set it away for morning cream, the children were put into their night clothes and allowed to tumble about a bit before being tucked up on a pallet in a corner with a quilt hung on chair backs to keep the light from their faces.

[73]

MILKMAID'S STAR

BLOCK SIZE:
6"
(15.2 CM)
SQUARE

Plenty of Quilts

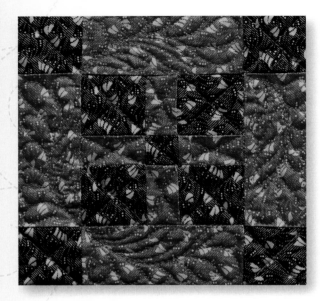

[25]

COMFORT QUILT

BLOCK SIZE:
6"
(15.2 CM)
SQUARE

Once more I essayed to go—the moon was shining and the way was direct, I had but to follow the fence line from their house to mine.

"Oh, but couldn't you stay all night?" urged Lizzie and I could see she meant it. "Please do!—if you can stand us."

"I expect her bed is more comfortable than we can make her," said the Optimist, tenderly regarding the wife's wistful face.

"Oh, but—" her lips trembled, "I haven't seen a neighbor woman since I left Mother. . . ." That settled it. I'd have slept on a tick stuffed with greasewood after that.

There were no room partitions as yet and only part of the roof was closed over. The bedsteads were still in their crates. But there was plenty of floor room and plenty of quilts. They "fixed up" a bed for me in a far corner and an open umbrella on the floor for a privacy shield. Lizzie had no nightdress to offer me for she had not been able to wash for so long that she was piecing out as best she could for herself and the children.

But I was learning! My lightweight, cactus-and-barbed-wire snagged, sun-faded khaki duster coat had been bought as an all-purpose wrap—and tonight it would serve the purpose perfectly.

While Memory Is Mine

There was one wash basin, very small, and I am sure I was the originator of paper towels for I made Lizzie laugh and groan as I utilized with entire success a clean piece of wrapping paper, urging her to try the other half. We giggled like girls. I forget how the brush and comb need was supplied. But I DO remember and shall hold in tenderest gratefulness while memory is mine, the sincere cordiality, the kindness in voices and eyes and generous sharing that made of plain food a banquet, the deep satisfaction of being with folks—real folks. It was all as simple and as natural and as "right as rain" and in that semi-arid desert rain was as right as God.

"You will come back soon?" urged the mother, clasping both my hands in hers. "I'm tied down some with the children but we'll be over when we can!"

"Come back *now*!" cried the little boy, as he and the mother watched me "do my stuff" under the lowest fence wire.

And they stood at the fence corner and watched me go, waving whenever I turned for yet another smile at my neighbors—folks—a woman—dear children—oh, thrice-blessed me!

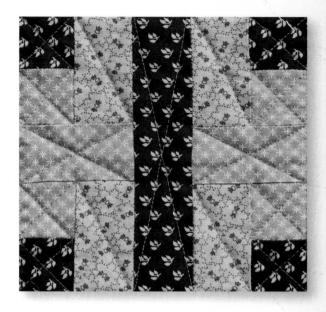

[33]

DOES DOUBLE DUTY

BLOCK SIZE:
6"
(15.2 CM)
SQUARE

A Fat Bundle of Mail

[65]

LOG CABIN

BLOCK SIZE:
8"
(20.3 CM)
SQUARE

The mail!—letters from friends, magazines and dailies with news of the "outside" world that seemed so far away and sometimes almost like a dream—how much we counted upon the mail! I was absolutely dependent for my mail on the thoughtfulness of others for I was long from Nesterville post office and my trips to the town could be but few and far between. Despite the kindness of neighbors and friends, I sometimes was weeks without mail and when the fat bundle came I was lost to everything else until the last word of the last letter had been read and reread, the papers scanned, and the magazines at least paged over to see what they offered.

At the time of which I am now writing, a young couple, Jed and Jennie Thompkins, nearly three miles west of me, picked up my mail whenever they or "he" went to town and kept it at their house until connections could be made more or less easily. Once in a great while, loose cattle, weather, mosquitoes and my own strength, all permitting, I could walk to their log house, either staying all night or being "run home" after supper behind Jed's frisky bronchos of which I was always deadly afraid.

Gave Her a Feeling

Jennie, Jed's pale, thin, sad-eyed young wife, under-strong, over-worked, cheated by early poverty out of the good education for which she had longed, daily cheated partly by ignorance and partly by continued poverty out of the nourishing food and daily rest she should have had, was as lonely for companionship as were all of us women pioneers. One day she humorously told me she had just eight good reasons for not coming to see me oftener: two tricky bronchos, two precious babes, and the four barbed wire gates that lay between her house and mine. But she did come once in a great while, notwithstanding.

On this particular day, looking over the accumulated pieces of my mail that had been long waiting for delivery to Cabin O'Wildwinds, she noticed a letter which, she said, "gave her a feeling" that there was something in it I would want to see as soon as possible. So, in the spirit of the true pioneer and good neighbor, she determined I should have it.

[60]

KIND NEIGHBORS

BLOCK SIZE:
8"
(20.3 CM)
SQUARE

Not-So-Simple Job

[86]

PERSEVERANCE

BLOCK SIZE:
6"
(15.2 CM)
SQUARE

Jennie could not walk with the children and she could not leave them. Jed was away for two or three days helping a neighbor but would be home that night and she knew he would want to rest instead of going to my place. So there was but one thing left to do—hitch up the bronchos and come to Cabin O'Wildwinds herself. Not so easy as it sounds!

First she had to bathe and dress the children and herself—a real chore, added to a morning of heavy and hurrying chores for she did the milking and other hard outside work when Jed was gone. Then, leaving the children in the house, she had to harness the tricky brutes, hitch them to the unwieldy wagon, lead them out and tie them securely outside the first of the four barbed-wire gates. This job completed, whatever of freshness she had felt from her bath and change of dress was gone; if she had hitched up and then dressed, the bronchos would have to stand that much longer and be the more nervous when she started out and they were "right up on their toes," as it was, having been idle for three days. Next, she brought the two children from the house, carrying the heavy baby girl and helping the toddling older child along. When the wire gate was closed, there was the not-so-simple job of getting the children safe into the wagon, the bronchos untied and herself seated with the reins well in hand for like most of the plains-bred-and-broken horses, these were "mean"—not to be trusted for a minute out from under an understanding and capable hand.

A Dangerous Business

The first half mile led across a wide and steep-sided coulee in which Russian thistles had piled up and where Jed, although the coulee was on his land, had let them stay—he was never quite equal to the heroic and many-sided job of farming a homestead. It was dangerous business, crossing that coulee, for the bronchos hated the prickly thistles and could hardly be persuaded to go ahead but Jennie was no mean horsewoman and she drove them to the task, although she was risking three lives when she did it. At the end of his half mile was a second gate to be opened and securely closed again, and to do this she had to get out, tie the bronchos, lift the children out and place them at a safe distance on the ground, open the gate, take the wagon through, tie the beasts again, get the children, close the gate, untie, drive on. Through the third gate, she repeated the process, after which came another half mile and then my gate, through which she did not have to come, as she could tie outside. I had seen her coming and met her, taking the baby from her over the top wire, while she and the little boy crawled through.

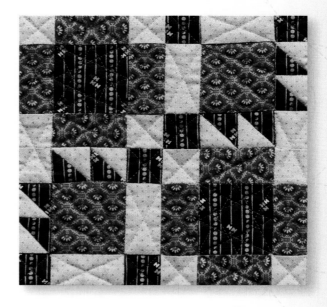

[11]

BLAZED TRAIL

BLOCK SIZE:
8"
(20.3 CM)
SQUARE

The Sack of Mail

[34]

ENVELOPE QUILT

BLOCK SIZE:
6"
(15.2 CM)
SQUARE

Delighted as I was to have a visit from Jennie, of whom I was very fond, happy though I was to have the mail, I could not refrain from remonstrating with her for making the difficult journey alone with the children.

"Oh, that's all right," she said quietly, wiping the white rim of alkali dust from her eyes and lips, and stooping to get hold of a spear of devil grass that had worked through her skirts to the tender skin. "If I didn't just pick up and go once in a while, I'd never get anywhere. Besides—I don't know—I had a feeling—don't you get such a feeling sometimes—I'd ought to come. There's a letter in there looks important. I always want my mail even if it's only a postal card."

After I had given her water to bathe her face and hands and had made a refreshing drink out of vinegar and the juice of some canned berries Mary had given me, I explored the sack of mail.

A Good Job Offer

"There," said Jennie, selecting one letter from the fat budget in my hand, "that's the one—open that first."

I wondered what there was about it that looked so important to her for I had an extensive correspondence and many of my letters were in "business" envelopes.

However, I obeyed, and opening the letter ran my eyes over the typewritten lines, Jennie watching my face. At first, in my haste to read, I did not take in clearly what it was all about and read it a second time.

"What's the matter?" asked my neighbor. "Nothing wrong is there? You got news? I *knew* it was news!"

"*News*?" I cried. "I should say it is news—more than news! Why, Jennie! What do you think? I've got—or I can get—a *job*! A good job on a magazine! Did you ever?" And with trembling voice and awed heart, I read the letter aloud. It was from the editor of a monthly magazine to which I had sometimes contributed, in a distant city—a member of the staff had been taken ill, they needed help, they had been "keeping tab" on my homestead experiment, they thought my knowledge of editorial work plus my added knowledge of country life would just fit me for the place. If I was free to leave, would I consider the matter?

[83]

OUR EDITOR

BLOCK SIZE:
6"
(15.2 CM)
SQUARE

World of the Printing Press

[9]

BELOVED SONG

BLOCK SIZE:

6"

(15.2 CM)
SQUARE

"But you've not proved up yet," said Jennie. "If you'd do that, you'd have to commute. Four hundred dollars is an awful lot of money to put on top of what you've already spent in fences and the house and all. And you wouldn't want to lose the place now you've stuck it out this long. What'd you have to do? Write stories for the paper? I couldn't do nothing like that! I wanted to be a teacher but I had to stay home and work. I couldn't have married Jed if Pa hadn't married again after Ma died. . . . Think you'll go? You've got a good lot of grass land and this is a right cute little house—you might be able to sell your relinquishment but there's no telling. Would you want to live in the city again? I wouldn't!" She talked along in her gentle monotone while I tried to get the import of the letter clear in my mind. Its message had brought to my inner hearing the always beloved song of the printing press, I could even smell the atmosphere of the composing room—gasoline, printer's ink, the sweaty bodies of the men at the stones. . . . Better than I should ever know the world of agriculture I knew the world of the printing presses.

What in the World?

Jennie's voice pattered along. "Of course, it'd be nice on some accounts. There'd be plenty of water right in the house," and the tired little woman sighed. "Gas and street cars and stores and all that. I've a married cousin lives in Cleveland in a flat—we visited her right after we were married. My, but that place was stuffy! And you never set foot out of doors unless you were going somewhere and then you had to dress up. They bought a half pint of cream every morning to do them all day and the vegetables from the market always seemed sta—*what—in—the—world!—*"

A squeal, a rattle, a crash out at the gate where the bronchos were tied. We rushed out. The brutes were rearing, plunging, kicking, biting—the wagon was over-turned. "Mind baby!" cried Jennie and was off on swift feet. I snatched the child from the bed, and with the little boy clinging to my skirt, followed as fast as I could. Just as Jennie reached the gate one of the team broke loose and tore madly away in the direction of home. The other had one leg fast between the barbed wires and was sawing it back and forth, tearing the wires loose and wrecking the gate. Both children were by this time screaming for Mother who was nowhere in sight, having disappeared behind the upended wagon. When she reappeared, she shouted to me to set the baby down, shouted to the little boy to stay beside sister, and called to me to help her.

[107]
TANGLED LINES

BLOCK SIZE:
8"
(20.3 CM)
SQUARE

The Wee Pioneer

[116]

WAGON WHEEL

BLOCK SIZE:
8"
(20.3 CM)
SQUARE

Jennie had the broncho by the bridle and in his frantic struggles to get loose he almost lifted her off her feet.

"There, Coaly, steady! Whoa boy! Whoa! Whoa! . . . If I had something to cut these wires—do you suppose you can help shift this wheel a bit—I don't dare let go of him—"

I told her I had a good wire cutter and plier at the house.

"Oh, get them, will you? Better take Babe back with you—Buddy, you stay right there by the fence until Mother gets Coaly loose. Tie Babe to something and leave her at the house—she'll be all right."

Back to the house I hurried, lugging the crying child, who kicked and struggled in my arms. No thought had I then of a "job!" My job was laid out for me—to do what had to be done and do it fast! I tied a soft rope up under the wee pioneer's arms, made the end fast to the bed leg, stopped long enough to drop a sprinkle of sugar on the little tongue curled up in screaming fright and put a sugary crust in the little fist, snatched up my tool-apron and ran back, stumbling over the cactus to the seat of war.

Coaly's Going Home

It made me turn cold to see Jennie so close to those wild hoofs but her face was calm, her eyes clear, her hands effectual, her head on her shoulders—a typical farm woman, efficient, ready for emergency change, to how it was done I do not know; I could do little more than stand by, hand tools, "take this," "hold that," "put that over here," "steady this"—but at length the imprisoned animal was freed, the flesh of one foreleg not much more than very badly scratched. Jennie tried to tie the nervous animal to a fence post but Coaly would have none of that, rearing, kicking, backing, so, knotting up the lines, she turned him loose to make his way toward home as he would, paused a minute to survey the smashed wagon, sighed, turned away from the wreckage and took her sobbing little son in her arms—arms that must have been aching with weariness.

"There! there!" she crooned. "You were Mama's little man," patting the small hot back. "See, Coaly's going home to tell Papa where we are and he'll come and then we'll go home and Mama'll make you some candy. Hush now! Sister's all alone up at the house—what do you suppose she's doing? . . . I had a big ironing to do this afternoon but I can't walk home and carry Babe and it's too far for this one to walk all the way. Besides there's an ugly old critter in our pasture and it wouldn't be safe to go through on foot—with the children—I've had enough fun to last me for one day! So I guess you'll just have to put up with us till Jed gets back this evening. The horses'll likely be in sight and he'll know something's happened and come hunting us. I'm awful sorry this had to happen to you . . . I'll help get the dinner."

[19]

CALM AND CLEAR

BLOCK SIZE:
8"
(20.3 CM)
SQUARE

The Money's the Thing

The happening had not been to me and getting a meal would be a distinct pleasure but it seemed a terrible thing that had happened to her and I said so. She shrugged her shoulders—she had come through worse, much worse, than this, she said. "The money's the thing," she added. "He'll have to buy him a new whiffletree and a new wheel, and maybe the other horse has hurt itself so it won't be able to work. Always something! Sorry your gate's torn up but I think I have the wire fixed so nothing can break in tonight. Jed can come over in the morning and fix it for you."

"Oh, I can do that myself," I said. "I've learned a lot since I took up this homestead."

"Yes," said Jennie, nodding, "you do when you're worth your salt—and *you* are!" That was a real compliment coming from the woman it did.

[106]

TABLE FOR FOUR

BLOCK SIZE:
8"
(20.3 CM)
SQUARE

A Quiet Old Plug

Toward evening, Jed came, pale under his tan and a little breathless.

"When I found Custer and Coaly at the fence I sure thought you were all killed!" he said, taking the children into his arms.

We told him what had happened.

"Sorry about your gate," he said to me. "There doesn't seem to be much of it left but I'll fix it up for you—we can stretch a wire across to keep stock out for the night. Custer hasn't a scratch on him."

"The wagon's in bad shape," said Jennie.

"Oh, well, I was going to get me a new one anyhow, and if the corn does well, old girl," he looked affectionately at his wife, "I sure am going to get you a quiet old plug and some kind of a light rig so you can take the kids and go when you've a mind to. But you've got to promise me you'll never take the broncs out again—just think—you might have all been killed!"

Jed stretched the wires across where the gate had been and then they went on their way across the fields, the father carrying the baby, the little boy dragging by his mother's hand. Pioneers!

[51]

HOME AGAIN

BLOCK SIZE:
6"
(15.2 CM)
SQUARE

Absent from the Land

[99]

ST. PAUL

BLOCK SIZE:
6"
(15.2 CM)
SQUARE

Two weeks later there came a very early and wholly unexpected killing frost and Jed's corn, still in the milk, thirty acres of it, on which so much more depended than "a quiet old plug and some kind of a light rig," was frozen. As I stood with Jennie in her kitchen looking out over the ruined crop, I wished that every city woman in the United States could understand as I was beginning to, what the farmers who raise the food for their tables have to face in weather uncertainty alone, and what farm women, even those on well-to-do farms, have to meet and bear and do.

The outcome of the letter Jennie had brought to me at such risk and cost, was that I availed myself of the Department's provision whereby homesteaders could be absent from the land during winter months, sent my beloved Lassie to a new home far across the plains—a prowling and hungry coyote had done this for Betsy Bobbett many weeks before—and turned my face toward the city for five months of employment.

Difficult and Delightful

For forty-four months I had lived alone in Cabin O'Wildwinds—for all that time had been water-rationed and held to a diet of canned stuffs, bacon and coffee; for forty-four months had tramped the plains in my big loose well-oiled boots, laced to the knees, worn rough clothes and gone bareheaded save in the wildest weather; for forty-four months I had companied with silence and solitude; how would it seem to be back in the rush and roar of the city; sit at a desk all day; use the telephone; ride on street cars; wear good clothes; eat seasonable foods; be among people; live by the clock; go to concerts and lectures; rarely see a sunrising; rarely if ever glimpse the stars? How would it seem?

It seemed—was—at once difficult and delightful. I began to discover how the long experience of homesteading had changed me from the woman I had been before. However, my "job" proved to be no small one and I was too busy to do much besides work at it. The five months' leave of absence was soon over. Turning steadfastly away from urgent and very attractive inducements to remain with the firm for which I had worked, I returned to my beloved wilds. I simply could not abscond—which meant selling my relinquishment or commuting—without further effort to make good. I could at least stay out the stipulated time and prove up.

[23]

CITY SQUARE

BLOCK SIZE:
8"
(20.3 CM)
SQUARE

Looked Good to Me

[98]

SPRING HAS COME

BLOCK SIZE:
8"
(20.3 CM)
SQUARE

izzie and the children gave me a heart-warming welcome and the Optimist shook my hand with a grip that said more than words. He had agreed before I left the previous fall to seed ten acres of oats for me, and he had kept his word. Stretching away toward their place I saw the ten acres clean of greasewood, rough grass and cactus. The seed was planted. Things looked good to me once more. I had a little money ahead for my second hay crop had been even better than the first and I had been able to save something every week from my pay check. Happily I put away my thin soled shoes and "city clothes," laced on the old cactus-proof boots and walked proudly out to view my quarter section. Before leaving them, the publishers had exacted from me a promise to go to them again the next winter. Life looked very livable. Gaily I set up my typewriter and sent a batch of hopeful letters to friends "back in the States" who never could see anything good in what I was doing.

It was a rare spring day. Early that morning I had found tiny spears of promise breaking through the soil of the oat field. I had rushed over to tell Lizzie and we had celebrated together—I believe she was as happy for me as she was for themselves when something good came their way for she was one of the big-hearted women who have room for others' joys and sorrows in their thoughts.

PART 12: BETWEEN TWO WORLDS

Thinking of You

But they were always somewhat concerned about me in my cabin, and Lizzie and I agreed on a distress signal system. Each evening we placed our lighted lamps so that each could see the other's. If I needed help in the night, I was to put two lamps in the window. I told her to do the same but she gently reminded me that there were two of them and it would be only a tremendous need indeed that would make them summon me out in the night. When there was a bad storm, we left our lights burning while it lasted, and the winking earth-stars would say to us, "Never mind! It'll soon be morning! Thinking of you!" In an unusual burst of storm or wind we sometimes signalled to each other, moving the lamps slowly up and down close to the glass—"Hello, there! Pretty bad, isn't it. Cheer up! It'll be over after a bit!" And so my nights were filled with peace, a sense of companionship, security.

[30]

DANGER SIGNAL

BLOCK SIZE:
8"
(20.3 CM)
SQUARE

I Dreamed

[63]

LIGHTNING IN THE HILLS

BLOCK SIZE:
8"
(20.3 CM)
SQUARE

One afternoon some time later another storm came up, this one an ever-welcome rain that settled down to a steady pour. I had every possible receptacle ranged along under the eaves and was gathering in a nice supply of soft water.

Toward evening the wind rose and the storm was wild indeed, the rain coming in gusts, the thunder and lightning seeming to come from all sides at once. I lighted a fire and enjoyed the coziness of the Cabin. I had brought back some new books with me. There was fuel in the house and food on the shelves and water coming down out of the sky to water the wild grass and the civilized oats. I was in a word-weaving mood and had an article in mind which I felt sure would sell. So while the day drew to a close, I dreamed—I was ever a good dreamer. If the oats did well, and surely they would, if that county road went through on my north line, as my locater assured me it would—if a few more, even two or three more—homesteaders located in my vicinity giving Lizzie and myself more neighbors and perhaps bringing us rural delivery . . .

A Bunch of Steers

In the midst of my dream, I looked out the window at the oat field—gasped with dismay: a "bunch" of more-than-half-grown steers were coming down the middle of the oat field—or ten big brutes—their horrible hoofs sinking deep into the rain-soaked gumbo. How they had broken in I did not know. That they must be gotten out and that as speedily as possible I did know—they would churn the seeded acres to destruction. I had no Lassie to help me for I had thought it best to leave her in her new home. So there was the situation—one woman on foot and a bunch of steers—a very tempest of storm, night at hand. I was a bit city soft. I rebelled. But there was nothing to do but get busy so I bundled up in my storm outfit, took a good club and faced my job.

First, without frightening the slowly moving, watchful, nervous bunch, I had to get to the gate nearly a quarter of a mile away and open it. Then I had to walk back, get quietly behind the brutes and head them for the gate, praying while I heaved one foot after the other out of the clinging gumbo that they would not take it into their several heads to break away in the opposite direction. How I did it I hardly know for they watched me as steadily as I watched them but somehow I kept them moving, quietly edging toward them so as to get them next to the fence at the other end of which was the open gate.

[15]

BROKEN PATHS

BLOCK SIZE:
6"
(15.2 CM)
SQUARE

Face Down in the Mud

[29]

COWBOY'S STAR

BLOCK SIZE:
6"
(15.2 CM)
SQUARE

The lightning blazed and the thunder roared, the wind nearly took me off my feet, the clinging, slippery mud was maddening, the rain beat on my face and ran down my neck.

Once for a minute the entire bunch got out of hand and then I ran at them, brandishing my big stick and yelling a cowboy *Hi-yi-yi!* until they were again bunched by the fence, headed for the gate. Once I caught my feet in a root and fell face down in the mud, one hand striking into a cactus clump as I fell and gathering in a beautiful crop of thorns. A greasewood thorn tore my cheek from ear to chin. I lost my hat. But I kept those children of Satan steadily moving away from the oats until they came to the gate. For some reason they did not like that gate and bunched there, bawling the matter over among themselves while I waited, almost exhausted, to see what they would do. With a sudden snort, as if to say, "Oh, what's the use—let's get rid of that critter that's following us!" heads down, tails flying, they plunged through the opening and away into the darkness of the open road.

I got the gate up and then, breathless, leaned my head on a gate post while the rain came down harder than ever.

Twenty Acres of Oats

here was still the long walk back to the house which was wholly invisible as I had not lighted a lamp before I left. But I made the trip successfully, guided by ceaseless lightning, got rid of wet clothes, made some tea and called it a day.

A few days later I proudly told the Optimist and Lizzie of my exploit. The good man complimented me on my pluck but there was an odd smile on his face as he listened. "You're still a tenderfoot though," he said, when I had told my tale, broadly winking at his wife. "I've been waiting ever since you came back for you to blow me up."

"Blow you up?" I echoed, puzzled. "Why, what for?"

"Haven't discovered that I planted twenty acres instead of ten?"

"Twenty!" I shouted. "But how perfectly splendid—oh, I'm so glad!"

"Well," he explained seriously, "I thought what was the use of making two bites of a cherry? Ten acres is such a little patch. So I told wife we'd pay for half the seed and I'd buy half the crop off you. If there's anything like a crop, you won't be out anything. Then I figured if you'd let me use the twenty acres again, I'd put it into winter wheat this fall—winter wheat does pretty well out here you know."

I was overjoyed and could have hugged the Optimist. I insisted, however, that I would pay for the seed—it meant so much to me to have the ground put into shape at almost no cost. He had his family to provide for—I had only myself.

[108]

TENDERFOOT

BLOCK SIZE:
6"
(15.2 CM)
SQUARE

Better for the Land

The growing weeks went by. Thinly, oh, how thinly, slowly, oh, how slowly, in straggly broken ranks the precious oat grass pushed upward. Slowly, sparsely, O ye God of all growing things, how sparsely, the stand headed out until at last it stood, fully but hardly worth harvesting. The honest Optimist looked the field over and though he sorely needed every grain he could gather in, he advised ploughing the crop under—it would be better for the land.

However, I insisted that he cut and haul it for feed—there was not enough of it to thrash. He estimated that it *might* thrash five bushels to the acre.

In spite of this disappointment, the Optimist still advised putting in winter wheat and as long as he was willing to try, I was more than willing to let him. The wild grass was faring poorly for after that rain on the night I turned the steers out, the weather had been dry as a bone—it looked as if my third hay crop would be a thin one.

[39]

FIELDS AND FENCES

BLOCK SIZE:
8"
(20.3 CM)
SQUARE

Tears of Thankfulness

At last the twenty acres were ready for the wheat and on one of those rose-and-gold mornings which made the plains a thing of beauty never to be forgotten, Lizzie and I put up a picnic lunch and with the children went out to see her good man sow the golden grain. Perhaps after all my dear dream of helping to grow "bread for the world" might come to something more than a dream. As we watched the sower ride up and down the field, the meadow larks rebuked unfaith with their songs of praise, the mountains upreared their frozen peaks to the smiling sky, a dear woman neighbor companioned me in my dream, an honest man was helping me in my struggle to make good. Tears of thankfulness filled my eyes and not even to the gentle, understanding soul beside me could I voice all that that hour of seed sowing meant to me.

[37]

FARMER'S FIELDS

BLOCK SIZE:
6"
(15.2 CM)
SQUARE

Cherry Pie and News

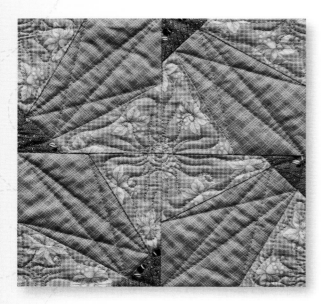

[46]

GOING EAST AGAIN

BLOCK SIZE:
8"
(20.3 CM)
SQUARE

For a second winter I had employment in the distant city. My friends, the Optimist and his wife and children, were as isolated as far as neighborly companionship was concerned, when I was away, as I had been before they had come but they were thankful that I could escape the bitter winter. And thankful indeed was I for the five months of employment and cash income, for my third hay crop was practically *nil* as the obnoxious weed, foxtail, spoiled what there was of it.

"I'm afraid you'll not come back to us in the spring," said Lizzie wistfully as we waited at the station in Nesterville for the train that was to take me east. "If the war should—continue—but how *can* it continue? And you'll write to us, won't you, what people in the city think about it?"

Lizzie was American born of fine old German stock. The Optimist was American. Lizzie was American in all her sympathies and loyalties but for all that, the things she was hearing said about the Fatherland of her own beloved and honored parents were not easy to hear.

First news of the breaking out of war overseas had reached me that summer of 1914 oddly enough. Mary Heathlowe had sent her youngest son, a twelve-year-old, over on horseback with a treat for me—nothing less than a cherry pie made from the last can of fruit she had canned on the home farm before coming to the new homestead. Ted and I were good friends and when the boy came he liked to linger and look over my books and study the maps I kept on the walls—he was "good in geography," his mother told me and more than commonly interested in events of the day.

The World at War

"Aren't you sorry the President's wife died?" he asked me casually. "We like Wilson at our house."

"Ted!" I exclaimed. "Tell me about it—I haven't heard. . . ."

"You haven't? Oh, then, maybe you don't know about the war either?"

"War? No." I turned to the map on the wall where, aided by the Chicago dailies which I received in smaller or greater batches according to how long my mail was held up at a neighbor's, I had kept geographical track of the unrest in central Europe. "Over here—in Serbia?"

"Yes! Over there—everywhere—Germany, Belgium, looks like the whole of Europe was going in—France, all of them. Pa says England's going to get what's been coming to her—I don't know what he means, do you? I like the English. Tennyson's English, isn't he?" Ted had wrecked the covers of my leather-bound *Idylls of the King* but it was worth it to share the boy's enjoyment of the tales. "Say," he offered, as the depth of my uninformedness impressed him, "I'll be over soon again—tomorrow or next day and bring you a lot of papers—Pa's been saving them."

But how could I wait for Ted's papers? That very afternoon, urged on by the boy's vague report of what was happening, I walked to Jennie Thompkins' for the accumulated mail. Not yet had she gotten the safe old plug and light rig, and she was keeping her promise not to take the bronchos out by herself.

[113]

UNREST EVERYWHERE

BLOCK SIZE:
6"
(15.2 CM)
SQUARE

Lessons and Strength

[49]

HARVEST HOME

BLOCK SIZE:
8"
(20.3 CM)
SQUARE

That night, having read till the print swam before my eyes, for the first time I felt clearly that my residence on the Great Plains could not be a permanent thing. I had been led to Cabin O'Wildwinds by an invisible hand for an inscrutable purpose—to learn lessons I needed to learn—to gain strengths I needed to gain—to "find myself" in a bigger and better way. Now the sway of events was tending to lead me away from the homestead. Several times Lizzie had reiterated her fear that the second winter away from the plains would finally cement my ties to the city but I had reassured her. I had to see the twenty acres of winter wheat mature and I fully meant to complete the required term of residence, proving up to the entire satisfaction of Uncle Sam. I had gone too far, invested too much, struggled with too many problems, overcome too many difficulties, to let everything go now.

So, while the war ravaged Europe, while Wilson faced the tremendous problem before him, while the pioneers endured the long winter on the plains, I sat at my desk, week after week, month after month, one side of my mind on my daily task, the other shuddering at the tragedy that was shaking all of the civilized world.

Tempted to Stay

Spring again and eagerly as any homing bird, again I turned my face west. Never had the west looked so good to me as then. "Blessings brighten as they take their flight." I had been offered a permanent position with the firm which I had served during two winters and had given tentative promise that if the proving up were satisfactorily concluded I would consider their proposition. But my heart of hearts was with the soil. If the twenty acres of winter wheat did very well indeed, I felt I might be tempted to stay on and with the Optimist's cooperation—for he said he would use more land if he could get it—enlarge the grain acreage. I was between two stools—I was inherently farmer-minded and a nature lover and though, by life-long experience habituated to the city and all her ways, I knew I should always be more deeply happy on the land. Well, we should see.

[13]

BRIGHT SIDE

BLOCK SIZE:
8"
(20.3 CM)
SQUARE

Looking at the Sky

[24]

COMET STAR

BLOCK SIZE:
8"
(20.3 CM)
SQUARE

As never before during that spring and summer the beauty of the wide plains thrilled me. Having overcome my tenderfoot fears and dreads, with good neighbors within more or less easy reach, my heart was at leisure to revel in the wonders of the unspoiled earth and the always matchless sky. Every hour of every day and night there was something new, something strange, wonderful, amazing, to see—only those with earthbound vision could fail to be enthralled. Said a woman who had stopped at the Cabin for an hour's sociability while her husband went to see A. Q. on some cattle business, staring out of my window, *Do you ever look at the sky?* By the expression of her face and the shallow dullness of her eyes, I knew she but seldom treated herself to that soul-enlarging exercise. Not so, the mistress of Wildwinds!

That sky! Across its vast screen moved an endless panorama which for variety, for grandeur, for witching beauty, fearful portent, for breath-taking exhibit of form and color, with play and interplay of rainbows, constellations, meteors, a comet even—the sky alone called me out of the house or to the windows regardless of time or task, day or night, not infrequently holding me spellbound until from sheer inability to "take in" anything more or stand up another minute I sought relaxation in some common humdrum household task. In that sky, I discovered the original source of all colors, glimpsed the models from which the old masters painted or carved mighty angel and tender cherub; found the source of Michael Angelo's inspirations and Dore's awful conceptions.

Sitting by the Hour

My favorite seat out-of-doors was a pine stump which no axe had been able to reduce to firewood. There I sat by the hour, watching as Day withdrew her regal garments over the western edge of the world, while at the same time—a sight no city nor any tree-cluttered country can yield—the Queen of the Night rose with imperial majesty on the eastern horizon: it was then dawn for the watchers beyond the western rim of the world and "dark o' the moon" for those across the eastern miles. I have stood still I dare not say how long, entranced, the North Star and the Dippers steel-clear overhead, the Rockies crouching like sleeping monsters, while the Morning Star like a flaming herald escorted the Sun up from his secret chamber—or was it the blaze of Aurora's crown as she brought "the light of day to men and to immortals" while the Moon sank softly out of sight on the opposite side of the horizon. I have caught my breath as meteors—on one memorable night no less than three at one time, sped in different directions to their unknown goals—not as townsmen glimpse a meteor briefly above their smoky roofs but moving in stupendous arcs, in majestically deliberate progress across the entire visible width of the star-gemmed dome. I have watched the play of distant storms—one, two, three simultaneously—in widely separated quarters of the heavens, down-pouring rain and hail, flashing lightning and the ensuing rainbows, all clearly defined, while overhead there was clear sky and every grass blade on the homestead was at peace.

[80]

NORTH STAR

BLOCK SIZE:
8"
(20.3 CM)
SQUARE

Was I Seeing Things?

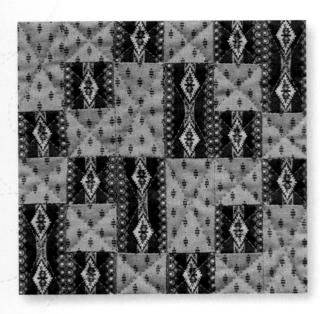

Now and then there was a breath of laughter amid the display of wonders. One morning as I was staring off toward the Optimist's house I saw something strange taking place in an intervening field. Was I "seeing things"? A fence, about a half mile away, beyond and near to which some cows were grazing, was moving—its posts seemingly elongating themselves into the air with a queer wavering motion that made me feel slightly dizzy. And between the rising posts, in a long thin line, there the plants that East Indian magic makes to grow before one's eyes. And the cows—they were growing, too, their legs ridiculously elongated. Of course, in a second or two I knew what it was—a mirage, the magic plants nothing more than the grass that grew along the fence line. Intently I watched the heat-made movie develop until the double picture was complete and as clear as a clear-cut photograph, the inverted image imposed on its double.

[74]

MIRAGE

BLOCK SIZE:
6"
(15.2 CM)
SQUARE

Wonders Out-of-Doors

About half an hour afterwards, I heard a step on the porch and there was A. Q., evidently a very much excited little man. "Say!" he shouted, as I greeted him, "did you see that there *mir*-rage? Good gosh! When I first saw it I sure thought I was drunk—only I don't drink! You saw it? What did you think?" His prominent blue eyes fairly popped with excitement.

"I didn't think I was drunk," I answered him laughing, "but for half a second I thought maybe I was a little off—up here!" tapping my forehead.

A. Q. shook his head seriously. "I don't wonder. It *does* get some people—this—" he looked across the plains searching for a word—"this everlasting *emptiness* . . . I never can see how you stand it. But that there *mir*-rage! I was eating my breakfast and it was so pretty outside that I took my coffee out-of-doors—I do that sometimes—it ain't right pretty *inside* my place. I was sitting facing that way and when them there cows began to go up and the fence along with them—good gosh! . . . Well, we had all about mir-rages and lots of other queer things when I went to school but, my land, I didn't believe every little thing I read. But if I hadn't 'v remembered what I'd read I'd been scared plum stiff this morning. I was wondering if you saw it, too!"

During that summer at Wildwinds, I improved every possible opportunity to fellowship with the Great Mother—never stayed in the house when I could be out-of-doors, seeking its wonders.

[82]

OPTICAL ILLUSION

BLOCK SIZE:
6"
(15.2 CM)
SQUARE

My Homestead Patent

[103]

SUMMER WINDS

BLOCK SIZE:
6"
(15.2 CM)
SQUARE

Through the spring and early summer—the wheat! From the first perceptible tinge of green that twenty-acre patch was to me the center of the universe. There were hours when I even forgot the War. The wheat was doing well—even A. Q. said so and he was no optimist, rather the opposite. Lizzie was happy with me. Her man felt quietly justified for his faith in the soil and gravely pointed out to me (for he was a God-fearing man), "if God Almighty can make a sinner's heart to produce righteousness, man, who is made in the image of God, can work until he can make poor ground grow something better than cactus."

It was while the wheat was "jumping" out of the ground that I went through the really thrilling process, at the county seat, of proving up and in due time receiving my patent for my homestead. It was a proud hour for me!

And an Armful of Quilts

My teacher friend, Alhambra, spent her vacation with me that summer—that summer of seven hailstorms, three of which were quite terrible enough but which came too early to do much damage to growing grain. The fourth storm descended upon us one afternoon when we were quietly reading and writing, trying to ignore heat and mosquitoes.

More alert to the vagaries of that wide world than my city friend, noticing a shadow creeping across the earth, I went outside to see what might be doing. Off toward the mountains was a strange cloud formation that looked like nothing so much as a gigantic grey blanket, rolled up loosely on the bias, one end of the great roll resting down on the earth, the whole moving steadily toward Wildwinds. I wondered if the end of all things was at hand. Inside of two minutes we were on our way to the tiny "cellar" out-of-doors—a mere hole in the ground, my friend carrying her handbag, I with the ever-ready lantern, matches and an armful of quilts.

Hardly had I dropped the pent's door above our heads when the storm struck and in another minute streams of water were pouring in around our feet and hail was battering on the frail boards close above our heads. We sat on grocery boxes, my friend shivering at the little field mice and fat grey-green lizards and enormous beetles that crept around us, while I, allaying her fears, wondered what was happening to my home.

[61]
LANTERN
BLOCK SIZE:
6"
(15.2 CM)
SQUARE

Bread for the World

[94]

ROARING HAIL

BLOCK SIZE:
6"
(15.2 CM)
SQUARE

As a matter of fact nothing happened and we need not have fled. Thoroughly chilled, muddy, glad to be alive, we left the hole in the ground and waded through the slimy gumbo back to the house while the sun came out and a vast rainbow of pulsating hues arched above the wheat.

The blessed wheat! It was doing splendidly and one day with my yardstick, while my friend laughed at my enthusiasm—she had not "fought, bled, and died," figuratively speaking, as I had for the hope of raising grain, "bread for the world,"—I went out to measure its height: fourteen inches and so far as I could tell, a fine lusty growth.

It was about a week after I had measured the height of the wheat, that Alhambra and I were awakened out of sound sleep in the middle of the night by a noise like machine gun firing, at first one sharp shot at a time, a few seconds between each, then a bombardment that was truly unbelievable. I got into bed with my friend but even with my lips against her ear could not make her hear for the roar of the hail on the roof and walls. We got up—lighted candles—I was afraid of the kerosene lamps. My companion was actually ill with fright and we were both shaking as in an ague. I ran to my emergency cabinet and we each took a heroic dose of old-fashioned Jamaica ginger and in a few minutes the fiery draught had brought our blood back to normal circulation. We gathered ourselves together as best we could, waiting and watching—we knew not for what. There was nothing to do—nowhere to go. Now and then a window pane broke but the house stood and the roof kept intact.

Heaven Help the People

At last the hail ceased as suddenly as it had begun and the first minutes of dead silence were almost as terrifying as the attack had been.

I went out on the porch and gathered a big pailful of huge stones, transparent spheres of compactest ice that had been hurled at us from the skies. I thought of Lizzie and her babes and went to the window with a lighted lamp—she was there ahead of me and neither of us moved the lights in our come-help-me signal—as we might have had to do had the events of the night been more terrible than they really were.

"This is the end of the wheat—the end of every planted thing—heaven help the people!" So we mourned and prayed as we lay down again to wait as best we might for daylight. We were out at dawn and I saw through hot eyes only beaten, bare ground where there had been twenty acres of greenest beauty—fourteen inches high. While I was standing there, my friend in mute sympathy beside me, what should I see but the Optimist's wagon with all of the family, coming our way. What had happened to them to bring them out at that hour? Heartsick I waited. I was afraid to have speech with them. Of course there was the slenderest possibility that their fields had escaped—hail is freakish in its ways. But their pale faces told me the story before they put it into words: "Wiped out—clean. And our best young mare killed. We were so anxious about you two—here alone in this little house—we just had to come over—we'll take you back to breakfast with us."

[97]

SIGNAL LIGHTS

BLOCK SIZE:
6"
(15.2 CM)
SQUARE

The Thought of Leaving

[48]

HARD TIMES BLOCK

BLOCK SIZE:
8"
(20.3 CM)
SQUARE

I had not lost my nerve during any of the storms nor during this dreadful night. I had looked with dry eyes at my denuded wheat field but as these blessed folk came into the house with us, the Optimist and Lizzie and I mingled our tears, not alone for ourselves and each other, but for all who had felt the cruel force of that phenomenal storm, and they were not a few.

I did not say it aloud to these dear neighbors just then but that night and that storm—which was but the fifth of the seven that terrified us that summer—brought me to the final decision to close the Plains chapter. It had been a marvelous chapter to me and the thought of leaving Wildwinds *hurt*. But it had to be—I could see that now.

As we drove back with them in the wagon to breakfast—they needed to minister to us as much as we needed their ministry—we could see the two sides of Cabin O'Wildwinds that had been exposed to the storm. The wee house had been an even, artistic, weathered gray—the battering hail had peeled all the gray away and the two sides shone in the sun like new lumber, yellow, over against the sodden field where there had been wheat, fourteen inches high.

Good-bye Cabin O'Wildwinds!

The next day I sent off a decisive letter to the city—I would accept the proffered position and leave Wildwinds to the care of the Optimist and his wife, giving him permission to do anything he liked with the land during the next year. Then came the packing up; good-bye words with neighbors and friends with whom I had shared the easy and the hard, the laughable and the tragic. Then the last morning with the Optimist's wagon at the door; the last lingering look around at the mountains and the land, the sky, A. Q.'s little hut, the far distant shacks here and there, the key in the door, the sob in the throat, the looking back and back and back, the Cabin out of sight, the shriek of an engine, the train—"Good-bye! Good-bye! God bless you!" The Adventure of Cabin O'Wildwinds was ended.

[69]

MEMORY WREATH

BLOCK SIZE:
6"
(15.2 CM)
SQUARE

Block Assemblies and Cutting Instructions

TEMPLATE NUMBERS & CUTTING
INSTRUCTIONS

[1] A SUDDEN TEAR

FINISHED BLOCK SIZE: 6" (15.2 CM) SQUARE

[2] AMERICAN HOMES

FINISHED BLOCK SIZE: 6" (15.2 CM) SQUARE

TEMPLATE NUMBERS & CUTTING INSTRUCTIONS

#2A, cut 1

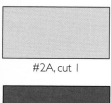

#2A, cut 1

#2B, cut 1

#2B, cut 1

#2C, cut 3   #2D, cut 6

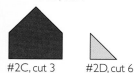

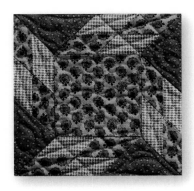

[3] AROUND THE CHIMNEY

FINISHED BLOCK SIZE: 6" (15.2 CM) SQUARE

TEMPLATE NUMBERS & CUTTING
INSTRUCTIONS

#3A, cut 1

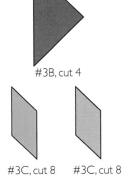

#3B, cut 4

#3C, cut 8   #3C, cut 8

[4] BACHELOR'S PUZZLE

FINISHED BLOCK SIZE: 8" (20.3 CM) SQUARE

TEMPLATE NUMBERS & CUTTING
INSTRUCTIONS

#4A, cut 5

#4B, cut 8

#4B, cut 4

#4C, cut 16   #4C, cut 20

#4D, cut 12   #4D, cut 12

140

[5] BACON PATCH

FINISHED BLOCK SIZE: 6" (15.2 CM) SQUARE

#5A, cut 4

#5B, cut 4

#5C, cut 1

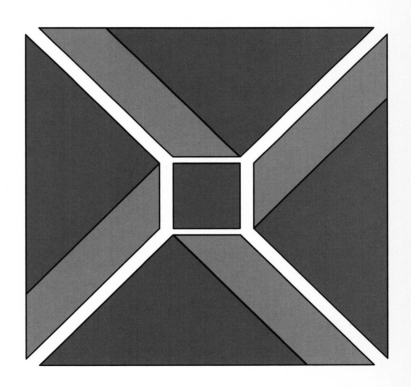

[6] BEACON LIGHTS

FINISHED BLOCK SIZE: 6" (15.2 CM) SQUARE

TEMPLATE NUMBERS & CUTTING INSTRUCTIONS

#6A, cut 1

#6B, cut 4

#6C, cut 4

#6D, cut 4

#6E, cut 8   #6E, cut 8

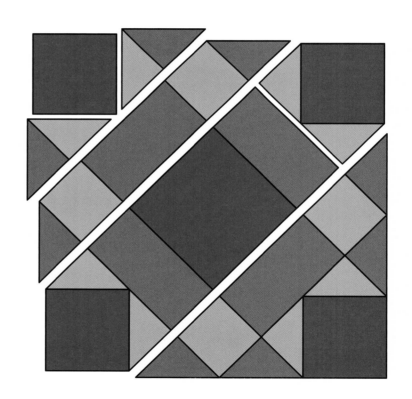

[7] BEG AND BORROW

FINISHED BLOCK SIZE: 8" (20.3 CM) SQUARE

TEMPLATE NUMBERS & CUTTING INSTRUCTIONS

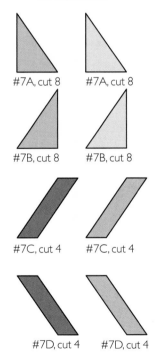

#7A, cut 8   #7A, cut 8

#7B, cut 8   #7B, cut 8

#7C, cut 4   #7C, cut 4

#7D, cut 4   #7D, cut 4

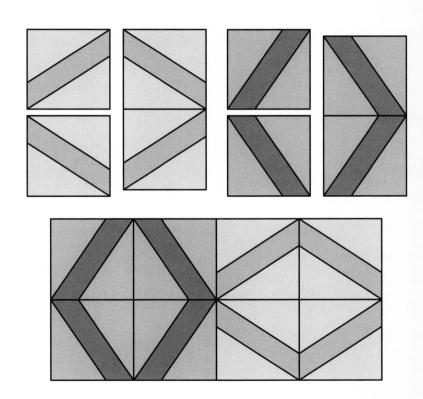

[8] BEGINNER'S DELIGHT

FINISHED BLOCK SIZE: 6" (15.2 CM) SQUARE

#8A, cut 4

#8A, cut 4

#8B, cut 16

#8B, cut 16

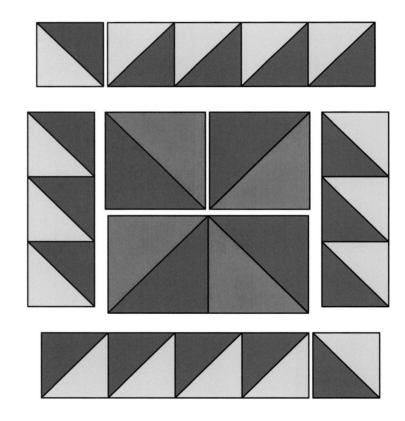

[9] BELOVED SONG

FINISHED BLOCK SIZE: 6" (15.2 CM) SQUARE

TEMPLATE NUMBERS & CUTTING INSTRUCTIONS

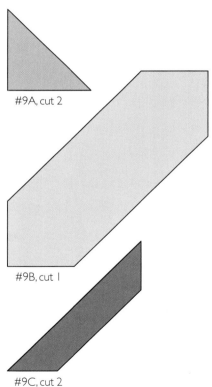

#9A, cut 2

#9B, cut 1

#9C, cut 2

[10] BITTER WASHPOT

FINISHED BLOCK SIZE: 6" (15.2 CM) SQUARE

TEMPLATE NUMBERS & CUTTING
INSTRUCTIONS

#10A, cut 1

#10B, cut 4

#10C, cut 4

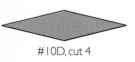

#10D, cut 4

#10E, cut 4

#10F, cut 4

BLOCK ASSEMBLIES AND CUTTING INSTRUCTIONS

[11] BLAZED TRAIL

FINISHED BLOCK SIZE: 8" (20.3 CM) SQUARE

TEMPLATE NUMBERS & CUTTING
INSTRUCTIONS

#11A, cut 2   #11A, cut 2

#11B, cut 8

#11B, cut 4

#11C, cut 6   #11C, cut 10

#11D, cut 8   #11D, cut 8

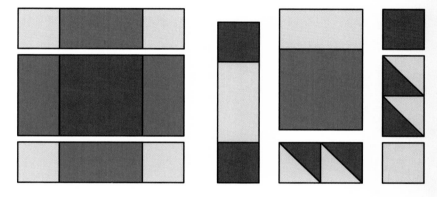

[12] BOX

FINISHED BLOCK SIZE: 6" (15.2 CM) SQUARE

TEMPLATE NUMBERS & CUTTING
INSTRUCTIONS

#12A cut 2

#12B, cut 2

#12C, cut 1   #12C, cut 1

#12D, cut 1

#12F,   #12F,
cut 1   cut 1

#12E,   #12E,
cut 1   cut 1

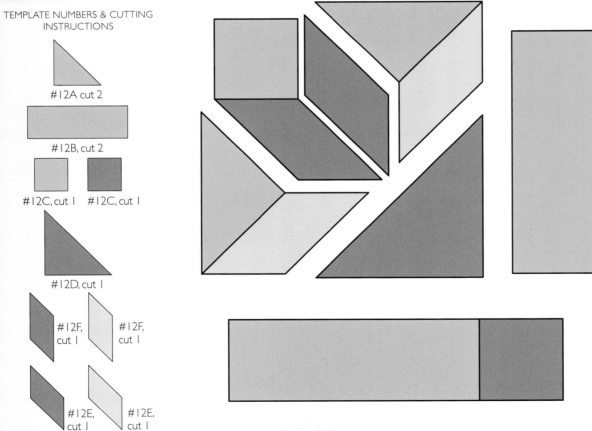

BLOCK ASSEMBLIES AND CUTTING INSTRUCTIONS

[13] BRIGHT SIDE

FINISHED BLOCK SIZE: 8" (20.3 CM) SQUARE

TEMPLATE NUMBERS & CUTTING INSTRUCTIONS

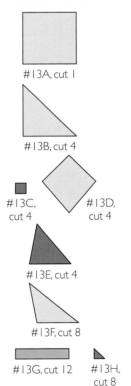

#13A, cut 1

#13B, cut 4

#13C, cut 4

#13D, cut 4

#13E, cut 4

#13F, cut 8

#13G, cut 12

#13H, cut 8

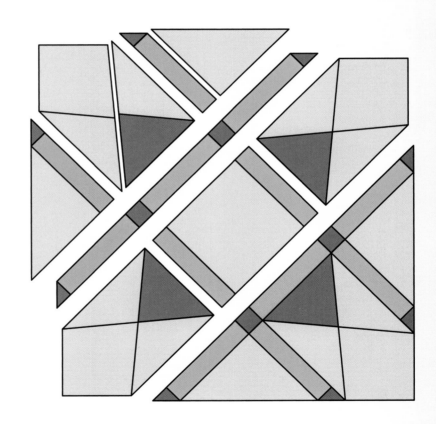

[14] BROKEN DISHES

FINISHED BLOCK SIZE: 6" (15.2 CM) SQUARE

TEMPLATE NUMBERS & CUTTING
INSTRUCTIONS

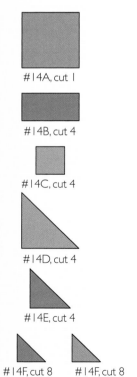

#14A, cut 1

#14B, cut 4

#14C, cut 4

#14D, cut 4

#14E, cut 4

#14F, cut 8   #14F, cut 8

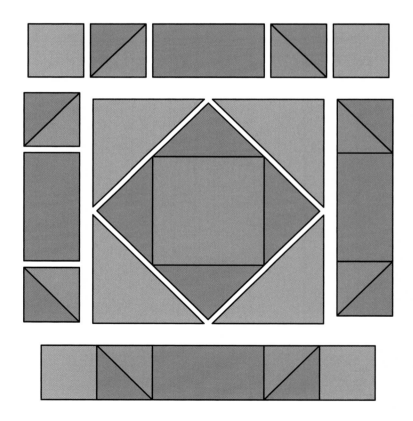

[15] BROKEN PATHS

FINISHED BLOCK SIZE: 6" (15.2 CM) SQUARE

TEMPLATE NUMBERS & CUTTING
INSTRUCTIONS

#15A, cut 4

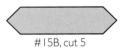

#15B, cut 5

#15C, cut 10

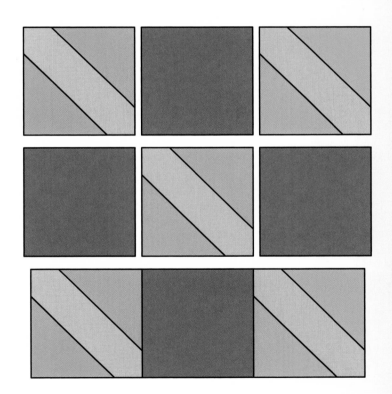

[16] BROTHERS

FINISHED BLOCK SIZE: 8" (20.3 CM) SQUARE

TEMPLATE NUMBERS & CUTTING
INSTRUCTIONS

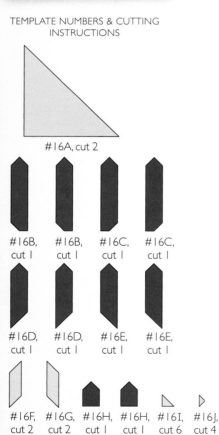

#16A, cut 2

#16B,
cut 1

#16B,
cut 1

#16C,
cut 1

#16C,
cut 1

#16D,
cut 1

#16D,
cut 1

#16E,
cut 1

#16E,
cut 1

#16F,
cut 2

#16G,
cut 2

#16H,
cut 1

#16H,
cut 1

#16I,
cut 6

#16J,
cut 4

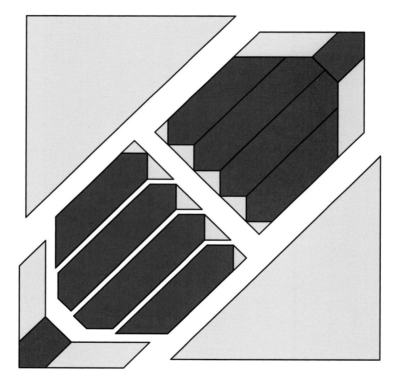

[17] BUILDER'S BLOCK QUILT

FINISHED BLOCK SIZE: 6" (15.2 CM) SQUARE

TEMPLATE NUMBERS & CUTTING
INSTRUCTIONS

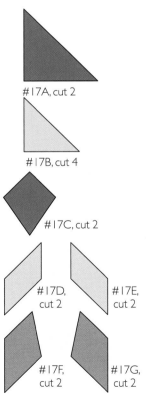

#17A, cut 2

#17B, cut 4

#17C, cut 2

#17D,
cut 2

#17E,
cut 2

#17F,
cut 2

#17G,
cut 2

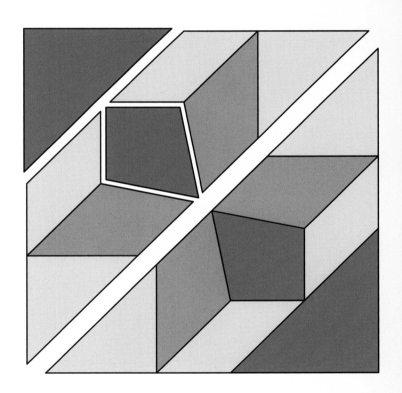

[18] CACTUS FLOWER

FINISHED BLOCK SIZE: 6" (15.2 CM) SQUARE

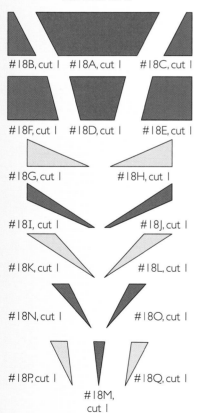

#18B, cut 1   #18A, cut 1   #18C, cut 1

#18F, cut 1   #18D, cut 1   #18E, cut 1

#18G, cut 1   #18H, cut 1

#18I, cut 1   #18J, cut 1

#18K, cut 1   #18L, cut 1

#18N, cut 1   #18O, cut 1

#18P, cut 1   #18Q, cut 1

#18M,
cut 1

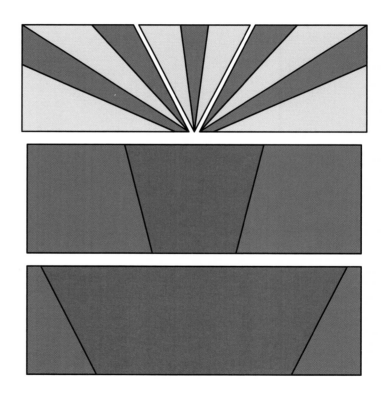

154

[19] CALM AND CLEAR

FINISHED BLOCK SIZE: 8" (20.3 CM) SQUARE

TEMPLATE NUMBERS & CUTTING INSTRUCTIONS

#19A, cut 1

#19B, cut 12   #19C, cut 4   #19D, cut 8

#19E, cut 4

#19F, cut 2

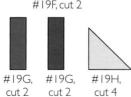

#19G, cut 2   #19G, cut 2   #19H, cut 4

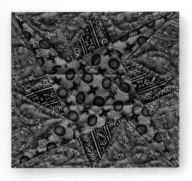

[20] CELEBRATION

FINISHED BLOCK SIZE: 6" (15.2 CM) SQUARE

TEMPLATE NUMBERS & CUTTING
INSTRUCTIONS

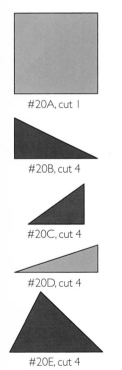

#20A, cut 1

#20B, cut 4

#20C, cut 4

#20D, cut 4

#20E, cut 4

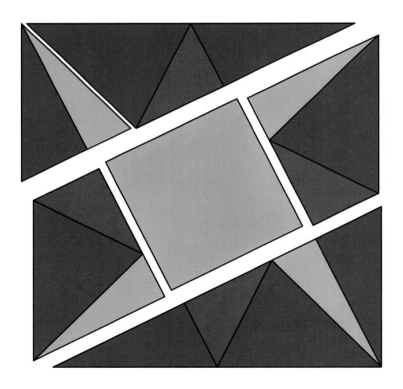

[21] CHICAGO STAR

FINISHED BLOCK SIZE: 8" (20.3 CM) SQUARE

TEMPLATE NUMBERS & CUTTING
INSTRUCTIONS

#21A, cut 4   #21B, cut 1

#21C, cut 4   #21D, cut 4

#21E, cut 4   #21F, cut 4

#21G, cut 4   #21H, cut 4

#21I, cut 8   #21I, cut 4

#21J, cut 8

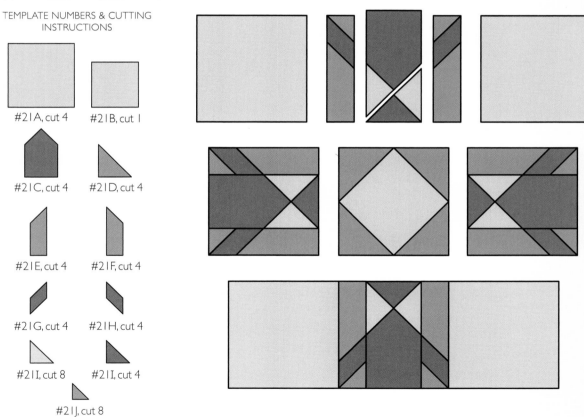

[22] CHIMNEY

FINISHED BLOCK SIZE: 6" (15.2 CM) SQUARE

TEMPLATE NUMBERS & CUTTING INSTRUCTIONS

#22A, cut 4

#22B, cut 4

#22C, cut 4

#22C, cut 1

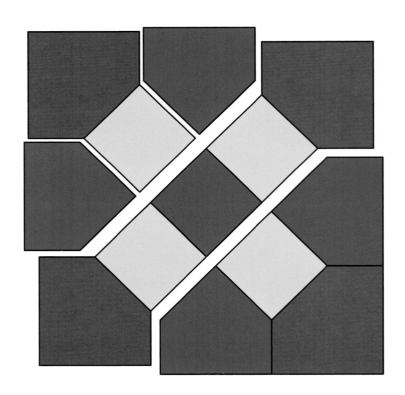

[23] CITY SQUARE

FINISHED BLOCK SIZE: 8" (20.3 CM) SQUARE

TEMPLATE NUMBERS & CUTTING
INSTRUCTIONS

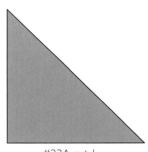

#23A, cut 1

#23A, cut 1

#23B,
cut 11

#23B,
cut 6

#23B,
cut 5

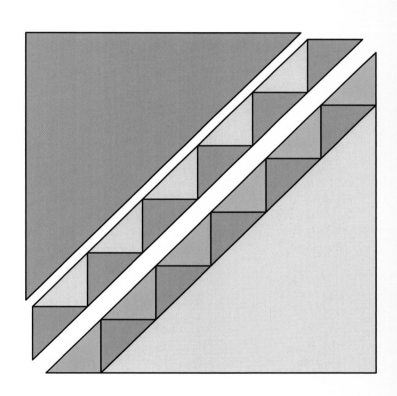

[24] COMET STAR

FINISHED BLOCK SIZE: 8" (20.3 CM) SQUARE

TEMPLATE NUMBERS & CUTTING
INSTRUCTIONS

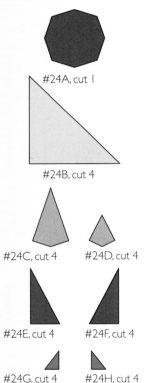

#24A, cut 1

#24B, cut 4

#24C, cut 4   #24D, cut 4

#24E, cut 4   #24F, cut 4

#24G, cut 4   #24H, cut 4

[25] COMFORT QUILT

FINISHED BLOCK SIZE: 6" (15.2 CM) SQUARE

TEMPLATE NUMBERS & CUTTING
INSTRUCTIONS

#25A, cut 4

#25B, cut 8

#25C, cut 4

#25D, cut 1

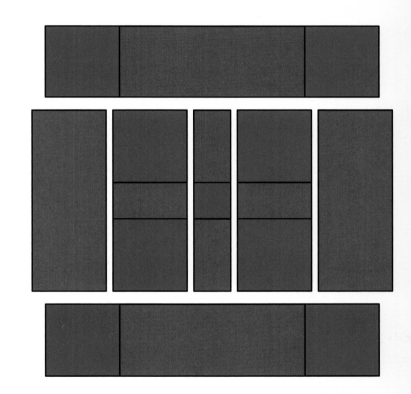

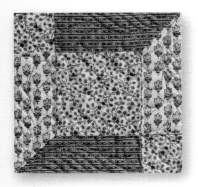

[26] COMPANY CAKE

FINISHED BLOCK SIZE: 6" (15.2 CM) SQUARE

TEMPLATE NUMBERS & CUTTING
INSTRUCTIONS

#26A, cut 1

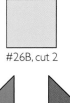

#26B, cut 2

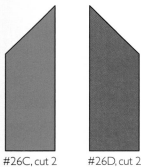

#26C, cut 2   #26D, cut 2

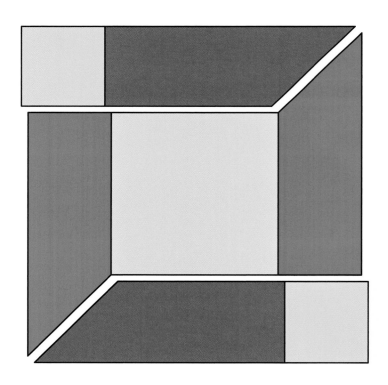

[27] CONSTELLATION

FINISHED BLOCK SIZE: 8" (20.3 CM) SQUARE

TEMPLATE NUMBERS & CUTTING
INSTRUCTIONS

#27A, cut 4   #27B, cut 4

#27C, cut 4   #27D, cut 1

#27E, cut 4   #27E, cut 4

#27E, cut 4   #27F, cut 8

#27F, cut 8   #27F, cut 20

#27G,   #27G,   #27G,
cut 8   cut 8   cut 4

[28] COUNTRY ROADS

FINISHED BLOCK SIZE: 6" (15.2 CM) SQUARE

#28A, cut 8

#28B, cut 16

#28C, cut 4

#28D, cut 9   #28D, cut 4

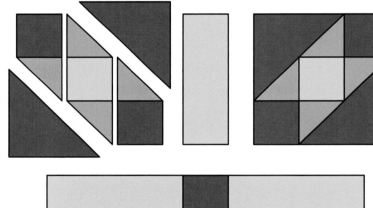

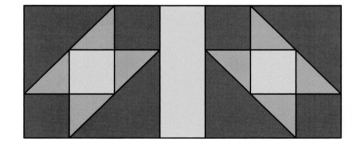

[29] COWBOY'S STAR

FINISHED BLOCK SIZE: 6" (15.2 CM) SQUARE

TEMPLATE NUMBERS & CUTTING INSTRUCTIONS

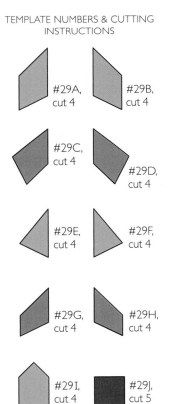

#29A, cut 4

#29B, cut 4

#29C, cut 4

#29D, cut 4

#29E, cut 4

#29F, cut 4

#29G, cut 4

#29H, cut 4

#29I, cut 4

#29J, cut 5

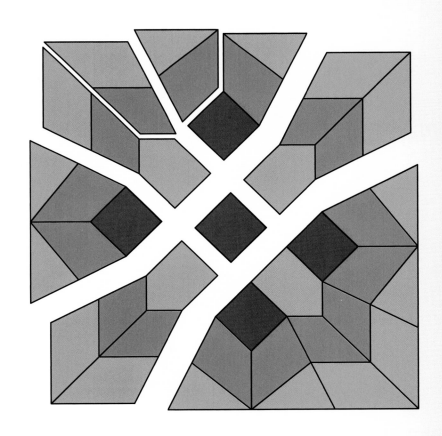

[30] DANGER SIGNAL

FINISHED BLOCK SIZE: 8" (20.3 CM) SQUARE

TEMPLATE NUMBERS & CUTTING INSTRUCTIONS

#30A, cut 8

#30B, cut 20

#30C, cut 44 #30C, cut 4

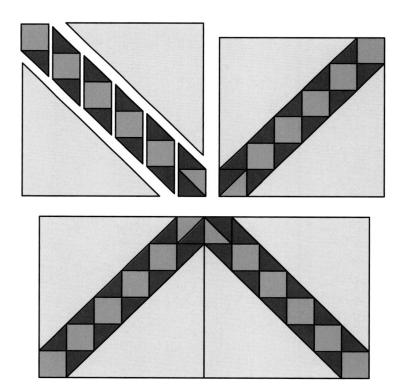

[31] DEJECTED ROOSTER

FINISHED BLOCK SIZE: 8" (20.3 CM) SQUARE

TEMPLATE NUMBERS & CUTTING INSTRUCTIONS

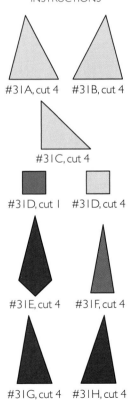

#31A, cut 4   #31B, cut 4

#31C, cut 4

#31D, cut 1   #31D, cut 4

#31E, cut 4   #31F, cut 4

#31G, cut 4   #31H, cut 4

[32] DESERT GARDENING

FINISHED BLOCK SIZE: 6" (15.2 CM) SQUARE

TEMPLATE NUMBERS & CUTTING
INSTRUCTIONS

#32A, cut 2

#32B, cut 8   #32B, cut 10

#32C, cut 2

#32D, cut 2   #32E, cut 1

#32F,
cut 1   #32G, cut 1

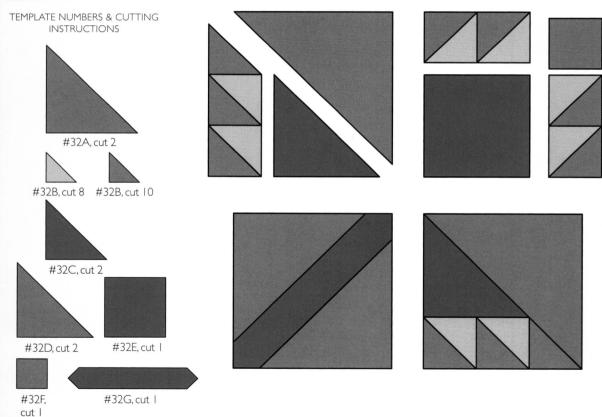

[33] DOES DOUBLE DUTY

FINISHED BLOCK SIZE: 6" (15.2 CM) SQUARE

TEMPLATE NUMBERS & CUTTING INSTRUCTIONS

#33A, cut 1

#33B, cut 4

#33B, cut 2

#33C, cut 4

#33C, cut 4

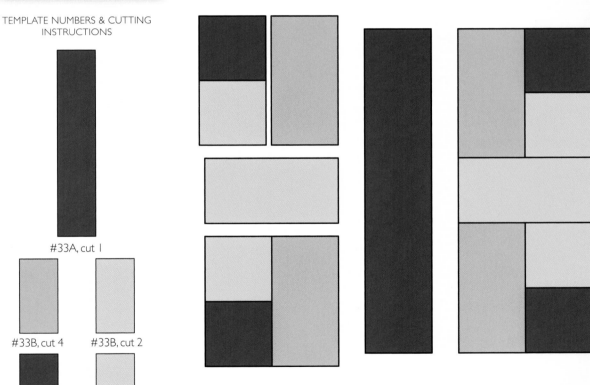

[34] ENVELOPE QUILT

FINISHED BLOCK SIZE: 6" (15.2 CM) SQUARE

TEMPLATE NUMBERS & CUTTING
INSTRUCTIONS

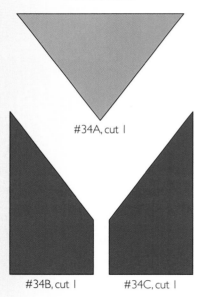

#34A, cut 1

#34B, cut 1   #34C, cut 1

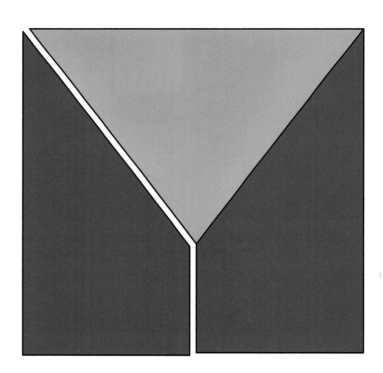

[35] FAR WEST

FINISHED BLOCK SIZE: 8" (20.3 CM) SQUARE

TEMPLATE NUMBERS & CUTTING INSTRUCTIONS

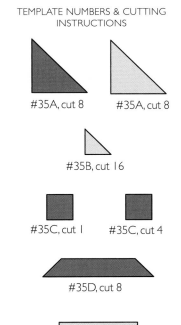

#35A, cut 8   #35A, cut 8

#35B, cut 16

#35C, cut 1   #35C, cut 4

#35D, cut 8

#35E, cut 4

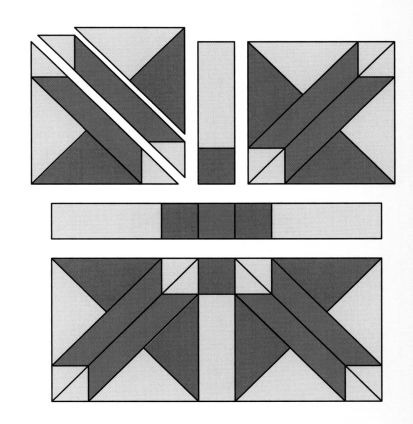

[36] FARM FRIENDLINESS

FINISHED BLOCK SIZE: 6" (20.3 CM) SQUARE

TEMPLATE NUMBERS & CUTTING INSTRUCTIONS

#36A, cut 1

#36B, cut 4

#36B, cut 4

#36C, cut 4

#36C, cut 4

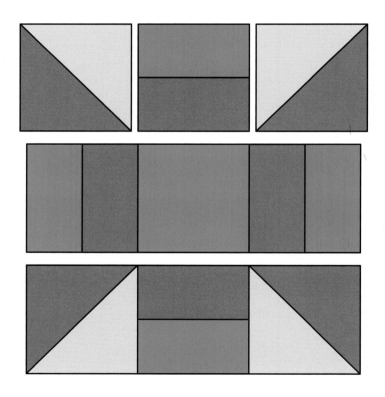

BLOCK ASSEMBLIES AND CUTTING INSTRUCTIONS

[37] FARMER'S FIELDS

FINISHED BLOCK SIZE: 6" (20.3 CM) SQUARE

TEMPLATE NUMBERS & CUTTING
INSTRUCTIONS

#37A, cut 4

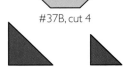

#37B, cut 4

#37C, cut 8   #37D, cut 4

#37E, cut 4   #37E, cut 4

#37F, cut 1

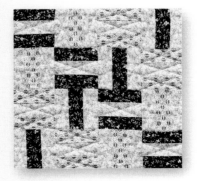

[38] FENCE POSTS

FINISHED BLOCK SIZE: 8" (20.3 CM) SQUARE

TEMPLATE NUMBERS & CUTTING
INSTRUCTIONS

#38A, cut 12

#38A, cut 12

#38A, cut 24

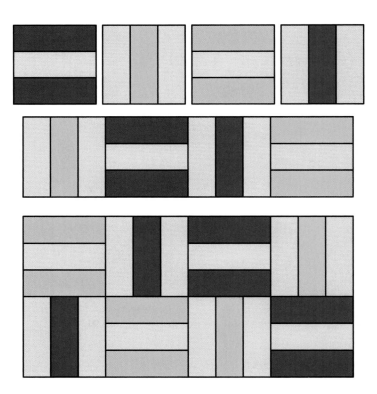

TEMPLATE NUMBERS & CUTTING INSTRUCTIONS

#39A, cut 1

#39B, cut 4   #39B, cut 2   #39B, cut 2

#39C, cut 8   #39C, cut 4   #39C, cut 4

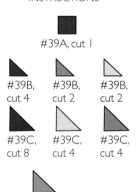

#39D, cut 4

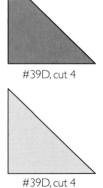

#39D, cut 4

[39] FIELDS AND FENCES

FINISHED BLOCK SIZE: 8" (20.3 CM) SQUARE

[40] FLAG IN, FLAG OUT

FINISHED BLOCK SIZE: 6" (15.2 CM) SQUARE

TEMPLATE NUMBERS & CUTTING INSTRUCTIONS

#40A, cut 2

#40A, cut 3

#40B, cut 4

#40B, cut 4

#40C, cut 4   #40C, cut 4

[41] FOOL'S SQUARE

FINISHED BLOCK SIZE: 6" (15.2 CM) SQUARE

TEMPLATE NUMBERS & CUTTING
INSTRUCTIONS

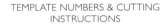

#41A, cut 4

#41B, cut 1

#41B, cut 4

#41B, cut 4

#41C, cut 12   #41C, cut 4

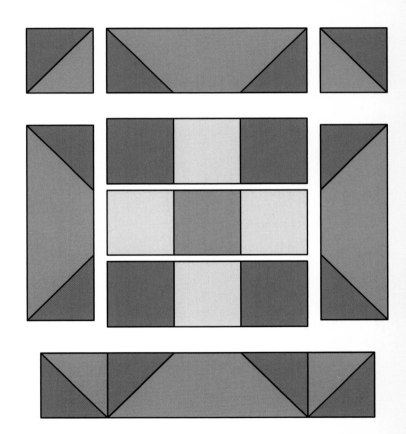

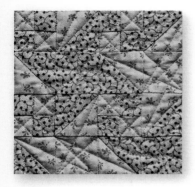

[42] FRIENDLY HAND

FINISHED BLOCK SIZE: 6" (15.2 CM) SQUARE

TEMPLATE NUMBERS & CUTTING INSTRUCTIONS

#42A, cut 2

#42A, cut 2

#42C, cut 8

#42C, cut 8

#42B, cut 8   #42B, cut 8

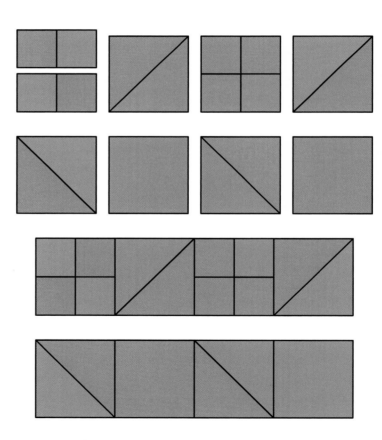

[43] FRIENDSHIP QUILT

FINISHED BLOCK SIZE: 8" (20.3 CM) SQUARE

TEMPLATE NUMBERS & CUTTING INSTRUCTIONS

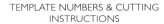

#43A, cut 4

#43B, cut 4

#43C, cut 2

#43C, cut 2

#43D, cut 2

#43E, cut 4

#43E, cut 5

#43E, cut 8

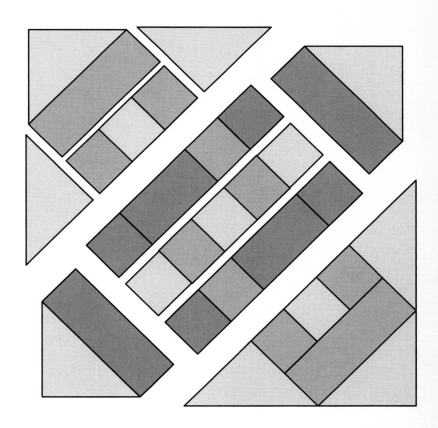

[44] GARDEN PATHS

FINISHED BLOCK SIZE: 8" (20.3 CM) SQUARE

TEMPLATE NUMBERS & CUTTING INSTRUCTIONS

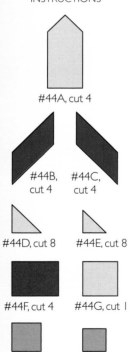

#44A, cut 4

#44B, cut 4   #44C, cut 4

#44D, cut 8   #44E, cut 8

#44F, cut 4   #44G, cut 1

#44H, cut 4   #44I, cut 4

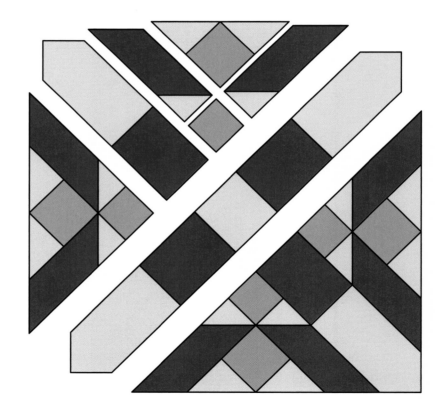

[45] GLOVE DESIGN

FINISHED BLOCK SIZE: 8" (20.3 CM) SQUARE

TEMPLATE NUMBERS & CUTTING INSTRUCTIONS

#45A, cut 4   #45B, cut 8

#45C, cut 1

#45D, cut 2

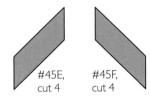

#45E, cut 4   #45F, cut 4

#45G, cut 4   #45H, cut 4

[46] GOING EAST AGAIN

FINISHED BLOCK SIZE: 8" (20.3 CM) SQUARE

#46A, cut 4

#46B, cut 4   #46C, cut 4

#46D, cut 4

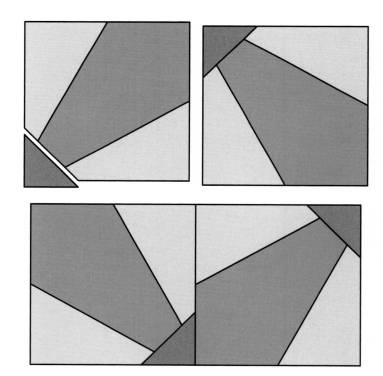

[47] GRANDMOTHER'S PUZZLE

FINISHED BLOCK SIZE: 6" (15.2 CM) SQUARE

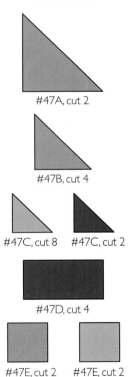

#47A, cut 2

#47B, cut 4

#47C, cut 8   #47C, cut 2

#47D, cut 4

#47E, cut 2   #47E, cut 2

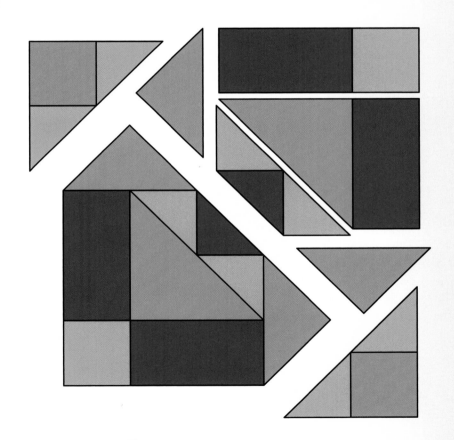

[48] HARD TIMES BLOCK

FINISHED BLOCK SIZE: 8" (20.3 CM) SQUARE

TEMPLATE NUMBERS & CUTTING
INSTRUCTIONS

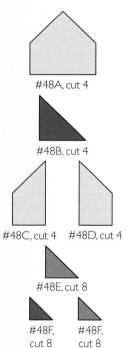

#48A, cut 4

#48B, cut 4

#48C, cut 4   #48D, cut 4

#48E, cut 8

#48F,   #48F,
cut 8   cut 8

[49] HARVEST HOME

FINISHED BLOCK SIZE: 8" (20.3 CM) SQUARE

TEMPLATE NUMBERS & CUTTING
INSTRUCTIONS

#49A, cut 4

#49B, cut 4

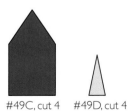

#49C, cut 4   #49D, cut 4

[50] HAYES CORNER

FINISHED BLOCK SIZE: 6" (15.2 CM) SQUARE

TEMPLATE NUMBERS & CUTTING INSTRUCTIONS

#50A, cut 2

#50B, cut 6

#50C, cut 4   #50C, cut 6

#50D, cut 2   #50D, cut 2

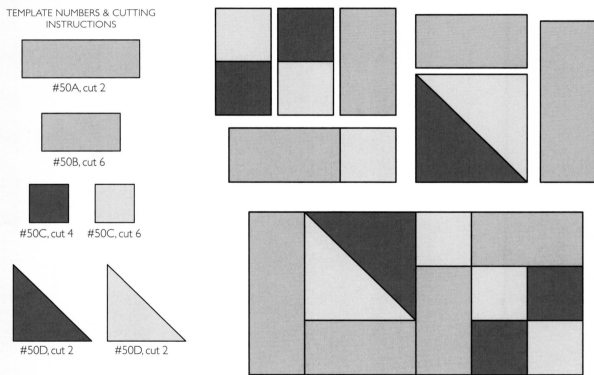

[51] HOME AGAIN

FINISHED BLOCK SIZE: 6" (15.2 CM) SQUARE

TEMPLATE NUMBERS & CUTTING
INSTRUCTIONS

#51A, cut 4

#51B, cut 8

#51C, cut 4

[52] HOMESPUN BLOCK

FINISHED BLOCK SIZE: 8" (20.3 CM) SQUARE

TEMPLATE NUMBERS & CUTTING INSTRUCTIONS

#52A, cut 1

#52B, cut 4

#52B, cut 4

#52B, cut 8

#52C, cut 4

#52C, cut 8

#52C, cut 8

#52D, cut 12

#52D, cut 4

#52D, cut 4

#52E, cut 8

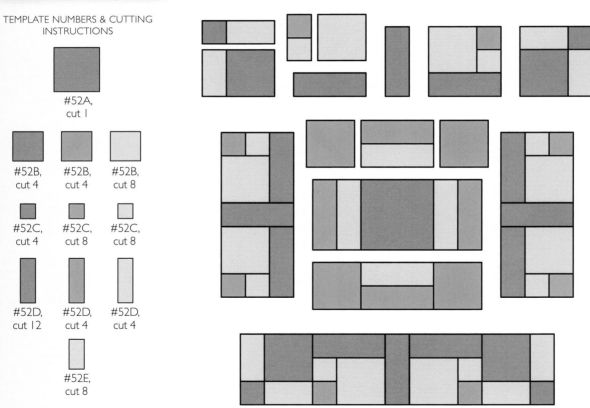

[53] HOPES AND WISHES

FINISHED BLOCK SIZE: 8" (20.3 CM) SQUARE

TEMPLATE NUMBERS & CUTTING INSTRUCTIONS

#53A, cut 4

#53B, cut 4

#53C, cut 4

#53D, cut 4

#53E, cut 8

#53F, cut 8

#53G, cut 1

#53G, cut 4

#53G, cut 4

#53H, cut 4

[54] HOUSEWIFE'S DREAM

FINISHED BLOCK SIZE: 8" (20.3 CM) SQUARE

TEMPLATE NUMBERS & CUTTING
INSTRUCTIONS

#54A, cut 4

#54B, cut 4

#54C, cut 4

#54D,
cut 4

#54E,
cut 4

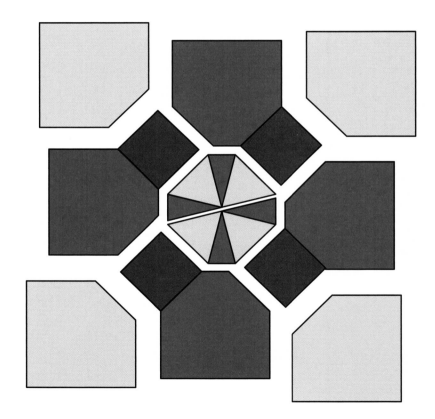

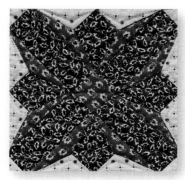

[55] IDLE HOURS

FINISHED BLOCK SIZE: 6" (15.2 CM) SQUARE

TEMPLATE NUMBERS & CUTTING INSTRUCTIONS

#55A, cut 4

#55B, cut 8

#55C, cut 4

#55D, cut 1

#55E, cut 4

#55F, cut 4

#55G, cut 4

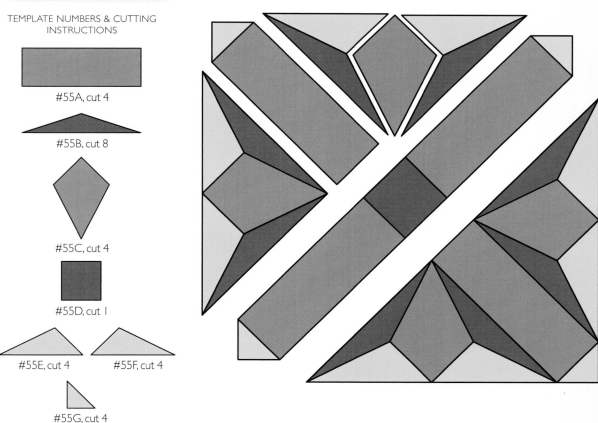

[56] INDEPENDENCE SQUARE

FINISHED BLOCK SIZE: 8" (20.3 CM) SQUARE

TEMPLATE NUMBERS & CUTTING
INSTRUCTIONS

#56A, cut 4

#56B,
cut 4

#56B,
cut 1

#56B,
cut 4

#56C, cut 4

#56C, cut 4

#56C, cut 8

#56D, cut 4

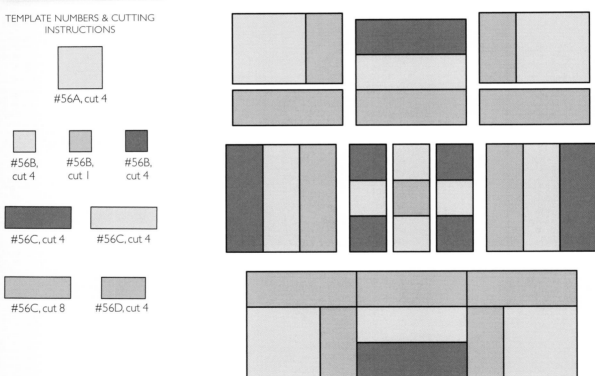

BLOCK ASSEMBLIES AND CUTTING INSTRUCTIONS

[57] INSPIRATION PATCH

FINISHED BLOCK SIZE: 8" (20.3 CM) SQUARE

TEMPLATE NUMBERS & CUTTING INSTRUCTIONS

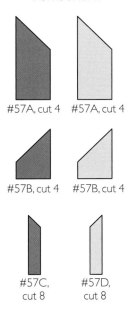

#57A, cut 4   #57A, cut 4

#57B, cut 4   #57B, cut 4

#57C, cut 8   #57D, cut 8

#57E, cut 4   #57E, cut 4

[58] KEPT FROM HARM

FINISHED BLOCK SIZE: 8" (20.3 CM) SQUARE

#58A, cut 4

#58B, cut 1

#58C, cut 4

#58D, cut 4

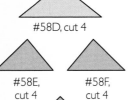
#58E, cut 4   #58F, cut 4

#58G, cut 4

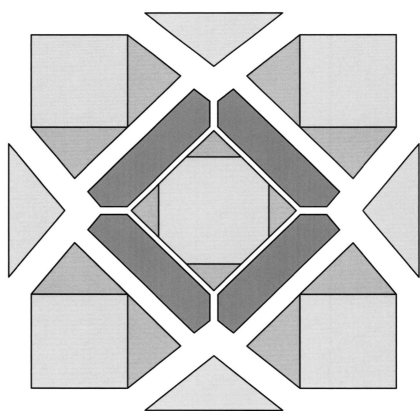

[59] KEYHOLE

FINISHED BLOCK SIZE: 6" (15.2 CM) SQUARE

TEMPLATE NUMBERS & CUTTING
INSTRUCTIONS

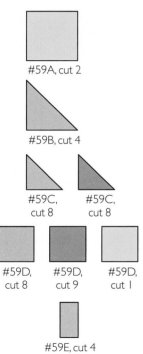

#59A, cut 2

#59B, cut 4

#59C,
cut 8

#59C,
cut 8

#59D,
cut 8

#59D,
cut 9

#59D,
cut 1

#59E, cut 4

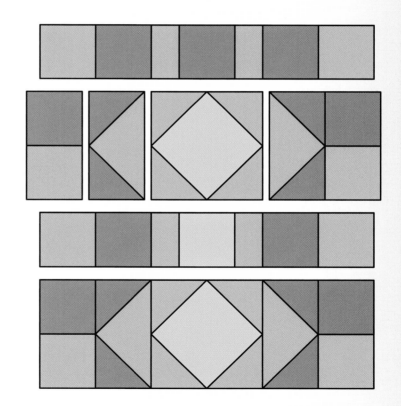

[60] KIND NEIGHBORS

FINISHED BLOCK SIZE: 8" (20.3 CM) SQUARE

TEMPLATE NUMBERS & CUTTING INSTRUCTIONS

#60A, cut 4

#60B, cut 4   #60B, cut 8

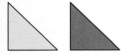

#60B, cut 4

#60C, cut 4   #60C, cut 16   #60C, cut 16

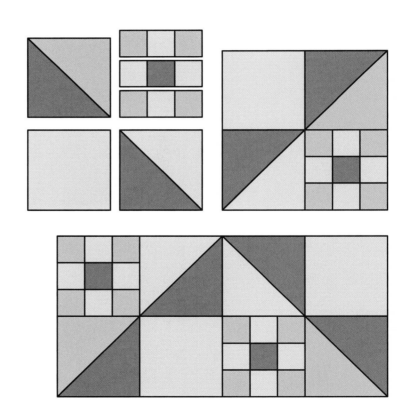

[61] LANTERN

FINISHED BLOCK SIZE: 6" (15.2 CM) SQUARE

TEMPLATE NUMBERS & CUTTING INSTRUCTIONS

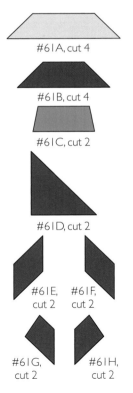

#61A, cut 4

#61B, cut 4

#61C, cut 2

#61D, cut 2

#61E, cut 2

#61F, cut 2

#61G, cut 2

#61H, cut 2

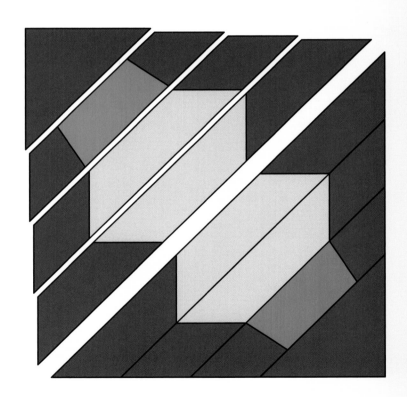

[62] LIGHT AND SHADOWS

FINISHED BLOCK SIZE: 6" (15.2 CM) SQUARE

TEMPLATE NUMBERS & CUTTING INSTRUCTIONS

#62A, cut 2

#62A, cut 2

#62B, cut 1

#62B, cut 2

#62B, cut 5

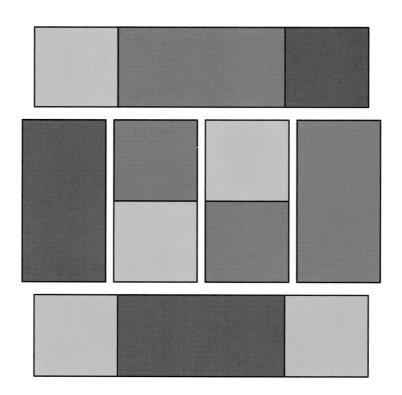

BLOCK ASSEMBLIES AND CUTTING INSTRUCTIONS

[63] LIGHTNING IN THE HILLS

FINISHED BLOCK SIZE: 8" (20.3 CM) SQUARE

TEMPLATE NUMBERS & CUTTING INSTRUCTIONS

#63A, cut 1

#63B, cut 4

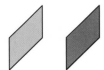

#63C, cut 8   #63C, cut 4

#63D, cut 4   #63E, cut 12

#63E, cut 12   #63E, cut 4

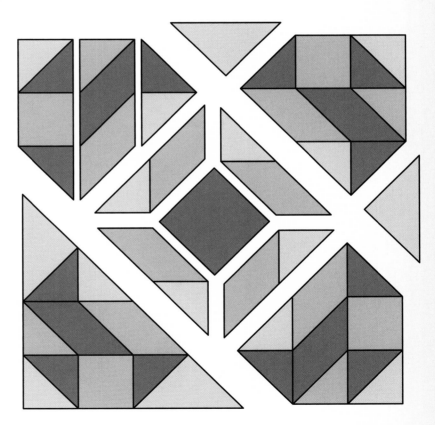

[64] LITTLE RAVEN

FINISHED BLOCK SIZE: 6" (15.2 CM) SQUARE

TEMPLATE NUMBERS & CUTTING INSTRUCTIONS

#64A, cut 4

#64B, cut 8

#64C, cut 16   #64C, cut 8

#64D, cut 1

#64E, cut 4

[65] LOG CABIN

FINISHED BLOCK SIZE: 8" (20.3 CM) SQUARE

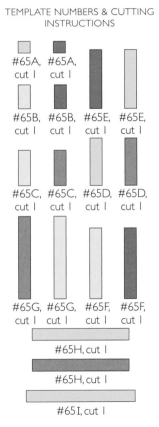

#65A,
cut I
#65A,
cut I

#65B,
cut I
#65B,
cut I
#65E,
cut I
#65E,
cut I

#65C,
cut I
#65C,
cut I
#65D,
cut I
#65D,
cut I

#65G,
cut I
#65G,
cut I
#65F,
cut I
#65F,
cut I

#65H, cut I

#65H, cut I

#65I, cut I

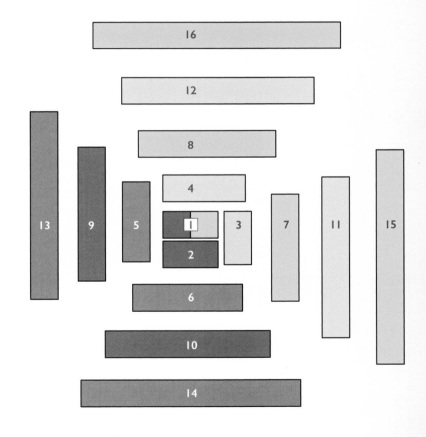

[66] LONELINESS

FINISHED BLOCK SIZE: 8" (20.3 CM) SQUARE

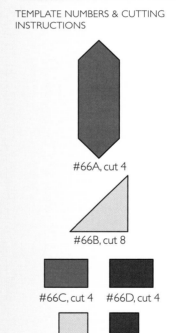

#66A, cut 4

#66B, cut 8

#66C, cut 4   #66D, cut 4

#66E, cut 9   #66E, cut 7

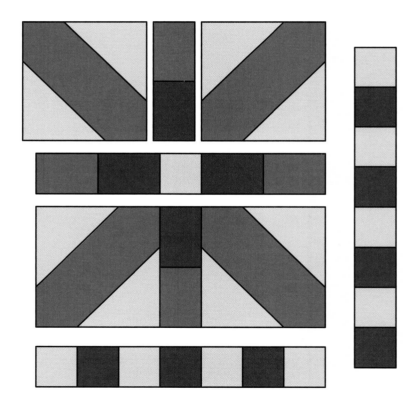

BLOCK ASSEMBLIES AND CUTTING INSTRUCTIONS

[67] MARY'S FAN

FINISHED BLOCK SIZE: 8" (20.3 CM) SQUARE

TEMPLATE NUMBERS & CUTTING INSTRUCTIONS

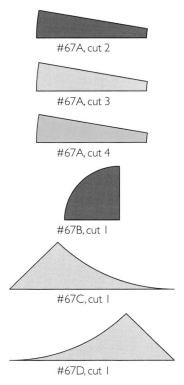

#67A, cut 2

#67A, cut 3

#67A, cut 4

#67B, cut 1

#67C, cut 1

#67D, cut 1

[68] MEETING HOUSE SQUARE

FINISHED BLOCK SIZE: 8" (20.3 CM) SQUARE

TEMPLATE NUMBERS & CUTTING
INSTRUCTIONS

#68A, cut 4

#68A, cut 4

#68B, cut 8

#68B, cut 8

#68C, cut 32

#68D,
cut 24

#68D,
cut 5

#68D,
cut 4

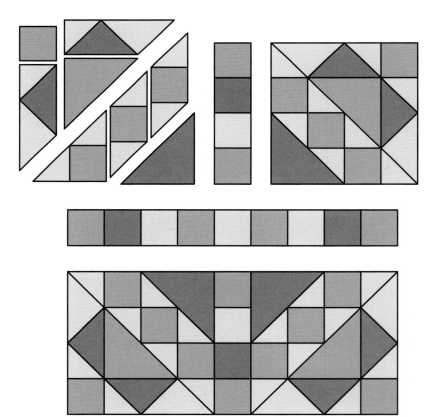

[69] MEMORY WREATH

FINISHED BLOCK SIZE: 6" (15.2 CM) SQUARE

TEMPLATE NUMBERS & CUTTING
INSTRUCTIONS

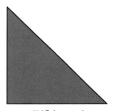

#69A, cut 4

#69B, cut 4

#69C, cut 4   #69C, cut 12

#69D, cut 1

[70] MEMORY'S CHAIN

FINISHED BLOCK SIZE: 8" (20.3 CM) SQUARE

TEMPLATE NUMBERS & CUTTING INSTRUCTIONS

#70A, cut 1

#70B, cut 8   #70B, cut 2

#70C, cut 8

#70D, cut 4   #70E, cut 4

#70F, cut 4   #70F, cut 2

#70G, cut 12   #70G, cut 12   #70G, cut 4

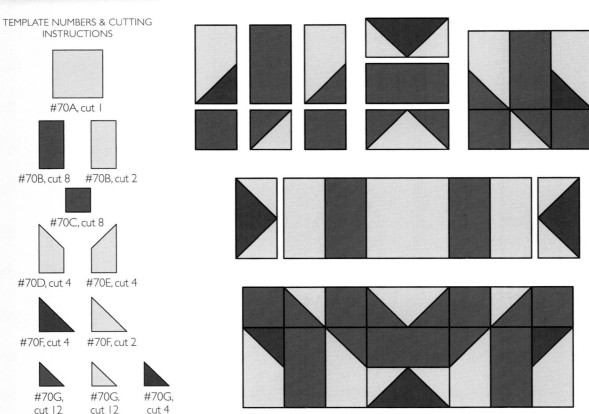

[71] MIDNIGHT CALLER

FINISHED BLOCK SIZE: 8" (20.3 CM) SQUARE

TEMPLATE NUMBERS & CUTTING
INSTRUCTIONS

#71A, cut 1

#71B, cut 4

#71C, cut 4

#71D, cut 8

#71E,   #71E,
cut 16   cut 24

[72] MIDSUMMER NIGHT

FINISHED BLOCK SIZE: 6" (15.2 CM) SQUARE

TEMPLATE NUMBERS & CUTTING
INSTRUCTIONS

#72A, cut 1

#72B, cut 4   #72C, cut 4

#72D, cut 8   #72E, cut 4

BLOCK ASSEMBLIES AND CUTTING INSTRUCTIONS

[73] MILKMAID'S STAR

FINISHED BLOCK SIZE: 6" (15.2 CM) SQUARE

TEMPLATE NUMBERS & CUTTING
INSTRUCTIONS

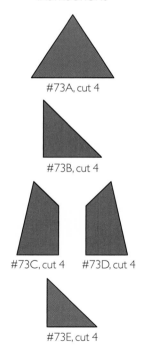

#73A, cut 4

#73B, cut 4

#73C, cut 4   #73D, cut 4

#73E, cut 4

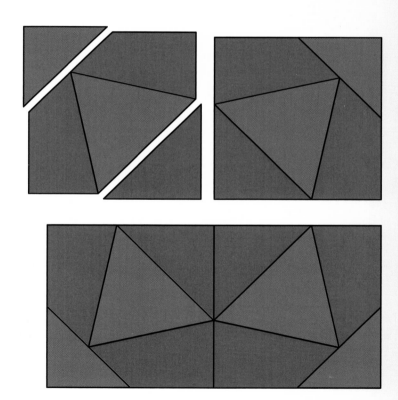

[74] MIRAGE

FINISHED BLOCK SIZE: 6" (15.2 CM) SQUARE

TEMPLATE NUMBERS & CUTTING
INSTRUCTIONS

#74A, cut 4

#74A, cut 4

#74B, cut 10

#74B, cut 10

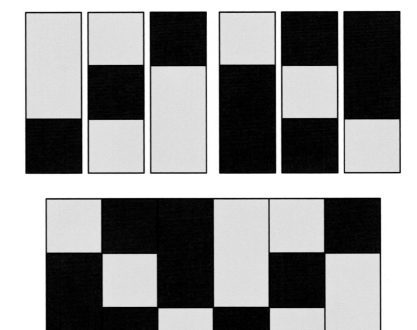

[75] MOON BLOCK

FINISHED BLOCK SIZE: 8" (20.3 CM) SQUARE

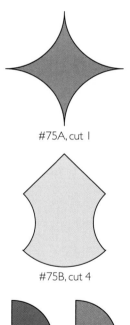

#75A, cut 1

#75B, cut 4

#75C, cut 4   #75C, cut 4

[76] MOTHER HEN

FINISHED BLOCK SIZE: 8" (20.3 CM) SQUARE

#76A, cut 2

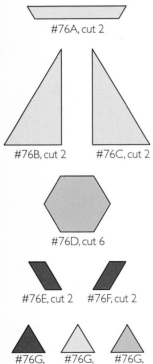

#76B, cut 2   #76C, cut 2

#76D, cut 6

#76E, cut 2   #76F, cut 2

#76G, cut 6   #76G, cut 6   #76G, cut 2

[77] MOWING MACHINE QUILT

FINISHED BLOCK SIZE: 6" (15.2 CM) SQUARE

TEMPLATE NUMBERS & CUTTING INSTRUCTIONS

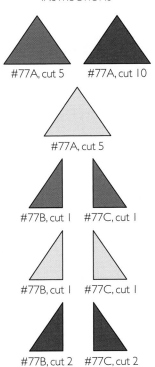

#77A, cut 5   #77A, cut 10

#77A, cut 5

#77B, cut 1   #77C, cut 1

#77B, cut 1   #77C, cut 1

#77B, cut 2   #77C, cut 2

[78] MY COUNTRY

FINISHED BLOCK SIZE: 8" (20.3 CM) SQUARE

TEMPLATE NUMBERS & CUTTING
INSTRUCTIONS

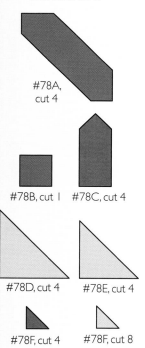

#78A,
cut 4

#78B, cut 1   #78C, cut 4

#78D, cut 4   #78E, cut 4

#78F, cut 4   #78F, cut 8

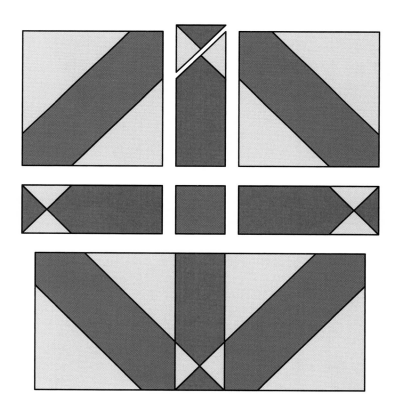

[79] NEED MY HELP

FINISHED BLOCK SIZE: 8" (20.3 CM) SQUARE

TEMPLATE NUMBERS & CUTTING
INSTRUCTIONS

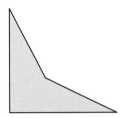

#79A, cut 4

#79B, cut 4

#79C, cut 4

#79D,   #79D,   #79D,
cut 16   cut 16   cut 16

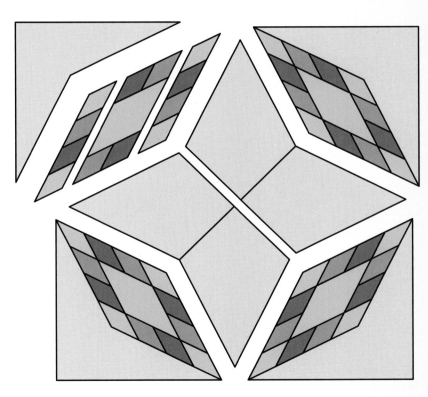

[80] NORTH STAR

FINISHED BLOCK SIZE: 8" (20.3 CM) SQUARE

TEMPLATE NUMBERS & CUTTING INSTRUCTIONS

#80A, cut 4

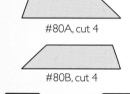

#80B, cut 4

#80C, cut 4   #80D, cut 4

#80E, cut 1

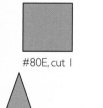

#80F, cut 4   #80G, cut 4

[81] OLD HOMESTEAD

FINISHED BLOCK SIZE: 6" (15.2 CM) SQUARE

TEMPLATE NUMBERS & CUTTING INSTRUCTIONS

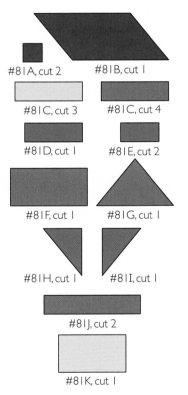

#81A, cut 2

#81B, cut 1

#81C, cut 3

#81C, cut 4

#81D, cut 1

#81E, cut 2

#81F, cut 1

#81G, cut 1

#81H, cut 1

#81I, cut 1

#81J, cut 2

#81K, cut 1

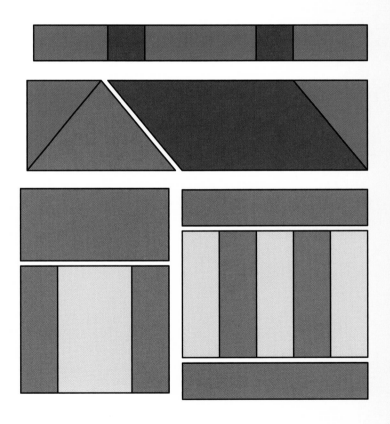

[82] OPTICAL ILLUSION

FINISHED BLOCK SIZE: 6" (15.2 CM) SQUARE

TEMPLATE NUMBERS & CUTTING INSTRUCTIONS

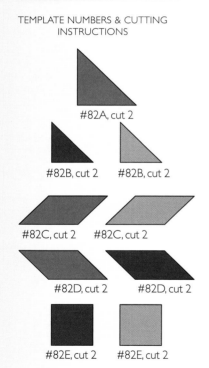

#82A, cut 2

#82B, cut 2   #82B, cut 2

#82C, cut 2   #82C, cut 2

#82D, cut 2   #82D, cut 2

#82E, cut 2   #82E, cut 2

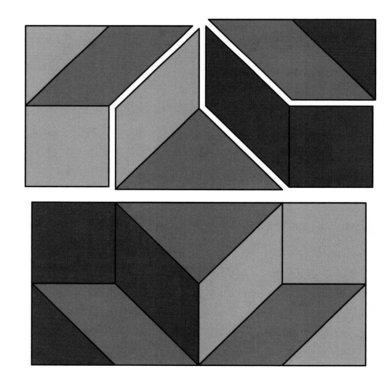

[83] OUR EDITOR

FINISHED BLOCK SIZE: 6" (15.2 CM) SQUARE

TEMPLATE NUMBERS & CUTTING INSTRUCTIONS

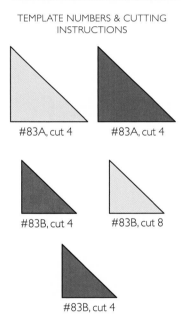

#83A, cut 4   #83A, cut 4

#83B, cut 4   #83B, cut 8

#83B, cut 4

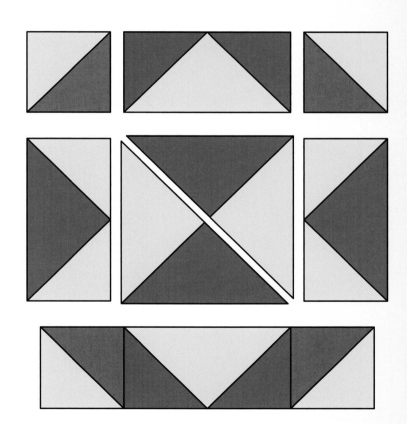

[84] OUT OF THIS WORLD

FINISHED BLOCK SIZE: 6" (15.2 CM) SQUARE

TEMPLATE NUMBERS & CUTTING INSTRUCTIONS

#84A, cut 4

#84A, cut 5

#84B, cut 1   #84C, cut 1

#84B, cut 2   #84C, cut 2

[85] PATCHWORK BEDSPREAD

FINISHED BLOCK SIZE: 8" (20.3 CM) SQUARE

TEMPLATE NUMBERS & CUTTING
INSTRUCTIONS

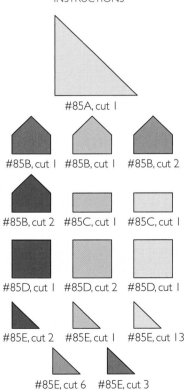

#85A, cut 1

#85B, cut 1   #85B, cut 1   #85B, cut 2

#85B, cut 2   #85C, cut 1   #85C, cut 1

#85D, cut 1   #85D, cut 2   #85D, cut 1

#85E, cut 2   #85E, cut 1   #85E, cut 13

#85E, cut 6   #85E, cut 3

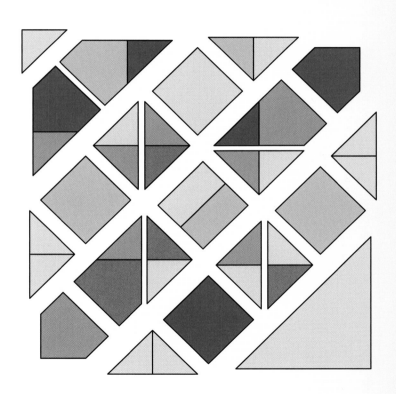

[86] PERSEVERANCE

FINISHED BLOCK SIZE: 6" (15.2 CM) SQUARE

TEMPLATE NUMBERS & CUTTING
INSTRUCTIONS

#86A, cut 2

#86B, cut 2

#86C, cut 2

#86D, cut 2

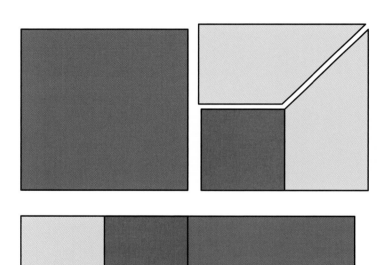

[87] PIONEER BLOCK

FINISHED BLOCK SIZE: 6" (15.2 CM) SQUARE

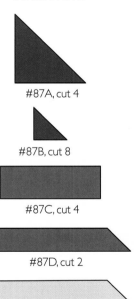

#87A, cut 4

#87B, cut 8

#87C, cut 4

#87D, cut 2

#87D, cut 2

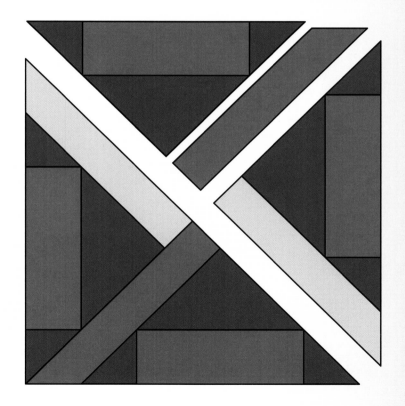

[88] POSTAGE STAMP

FINISHED BLOCK SIZE: 6" (15.2 CM) SQUARE

TEMPLATE NUMBERS & CUTTING INSTRUCTIONS

#88A, cut 1

#88A, cut 3

#88A, cut 2

#88A, cut 3

#88A, cut 3

#88A, cut 3

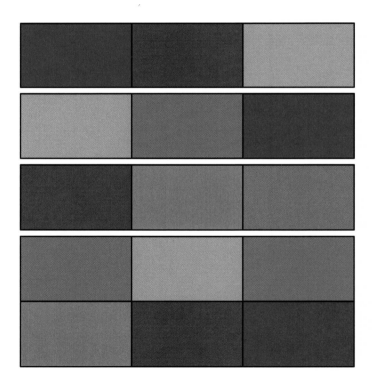

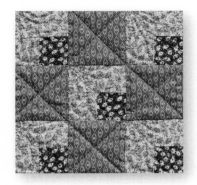

[89] PUSS IN THE CORNER

FINISHED BLOCK SIZE: 6" (15.2 CM) SQUARE

#89A, cut 4

#89B, cut 5

#89B, cut 15

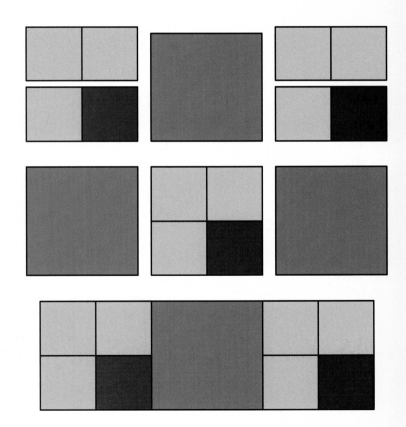

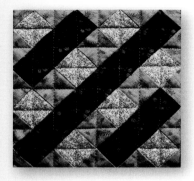

[90] RAILROAD CROSSING

FINISHED BLOCK SIZE: 6" (15.2 CM) SQUARE

TEMPLATE NUMBERS & CUTTING
INSTRUCTIONS

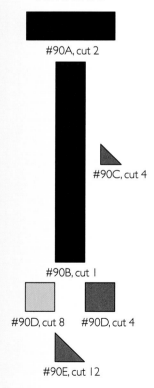

#90A, cut 2

#90C, cut 4

#90B, cut 1

#90D, cut 8   #90D, cut 4

#90E, cut 12

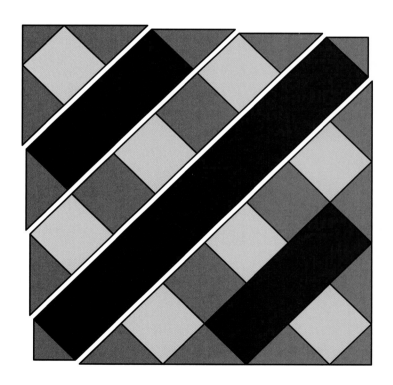

[91] RAINBOW BLOCK

FINISHED BLOCK SIZE: 6" (15.2 CM) SQUARE

TEMPLATE NUMBERS & CUTTING
INSTRUCTIONS

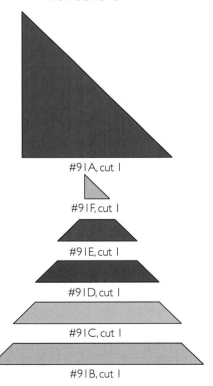

#91A, cut 1

#91F, cut 1

#91E, cut 1

#91D, cut 1

#91C, cut 1

#91B, cut 1

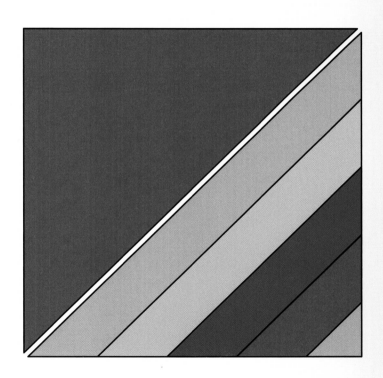

[92] RESIGNATION

FINISHED BLOCK SIZE: 8" (20.3 CM) SQUARE

TEMPLATE NUMBERS & CUTTING INSTRUCTIONS

#92A, cut 4   #92A, cut 4   #92A, cut 4

#92B, cut 6   #92B, cut 8

#92B, cut 10   #92B, cut 4

#92C, cut 4   #92D, cut 16

BLOCK ASSEMBLIES AND CUTTING INSTRUCTIONS

[93] RISING SUN, VARIATION

FINISHED BLOCK SIZE: 18" (45.5 CM) SQUARE
NOTE: A DETAILED PLACEMENT DIAGRAM IS INCLUDED IN THE ONLINE DOWNLOAD.

TEMPLATE NUMBERS & CUTTING
INSTRUCTIONS

#93A, cut 8

#93A, cut 8

#93B, cut 8

#93C, cut 8

#93D, cut 8

#93D, cut 12

#93D, cut 8

#93D, cut 4

#93D, cut 12

#93E, cut 8

#93E, cut 12

#93E, cut 8

#93E, cut 4

#93E, cut 12

#93F, cut 16

#93F, cut 16

#93F, cut 8

#93F, cut 16

#93F, cut 8

#93G, cut 8

#93G, cut 8

[94] ROARING HAIL

FINISHED BLOCK SIZE: 6" (15.2 CM) SQUARE

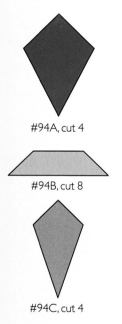

#94A, cut 4

#94B, cut 8

#94C, cut 4

[95] ROCKY MOUNTAIN

FINISHED BLOCK SIZE: 6" (15.2 CM) SQUARE

TEMPLATE NUMBERS & CUTTING INSTRUCTIONS

#95A, cut 1

#95B, cut 1

#95C, cut 1

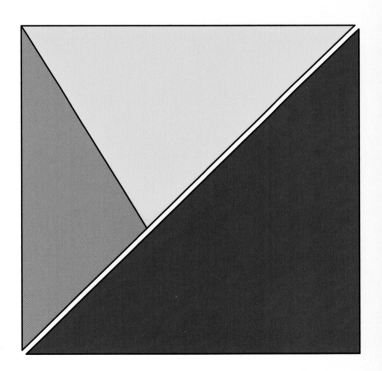

TEMPLATE NUMBERS & CUTTING INSTRUCTIONS

#96A, cut 1

#96A, cut 4

#96B, cut 4

#96C, cut 8

#96D, cut 8

#96E, cut 8

#96F, cut 4

[96] SAGE BUD

FINISHED BLOCK SIZE: 8" (20.3 CM) SQUARE

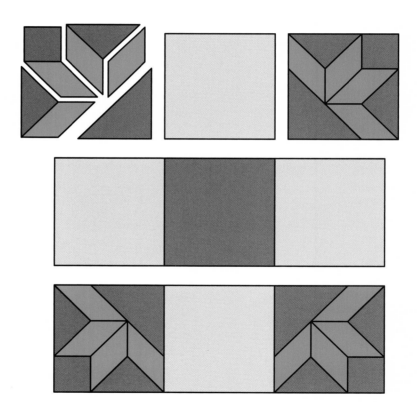

[97] SIGNAL LIGHTS

FINISHED BLOCK SIZE: 6" (15.2 CM) SQUARE

TEMPLATE NUMBERS & CUTTING INSTRUCTIONS

#97A, cut 1

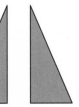

#97B, cut 4   #97C, cut 4

#97D, cut 4   #97D, cut 12

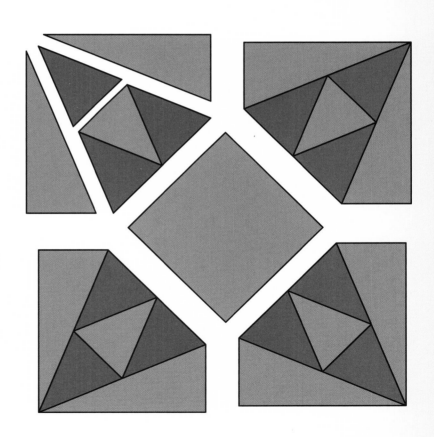

TEMPLATE NUMBERS & CUTTING INSTRUCTIONS

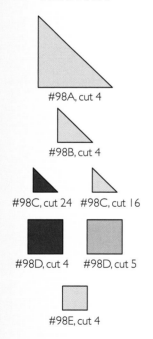

#98A, cut 4

#98B, cut 4

#98C, cut 24   #98C, cut 16

#98D, cut 4   #98D, cut 5

#98E, cut 4

[98] SPRING HAS COME

FINISHED BLOCK SIZE: 8" (20.3 CM) SQUARE

[99] ST. PAUL

FINISHED BLOCK SIZE: 6" (15.2 CM) SQUARE

TEMPLATE NUMBERS & CUTTING INSTRUCTIONS

#99A, cut 4

#99B, cut 4

#99C, cut 8   #99C, cut 4

#99D, cut 4   #99E, cut 1

#99F, cut 4

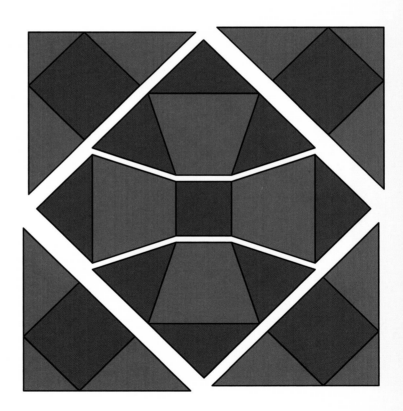

[100] STAR IN THE WINDOW

FINISHED BLOCK SIZE: 8" (20.3 CM) SQUARE

#100A, cut 8   #100A, cut 4

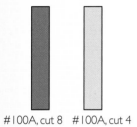

#100B, cut 1   #100C, cut 4

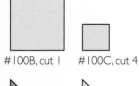

#100D, cut 4   #100D, cut 4

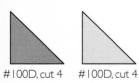

#100E, cut 4   #100F, cut 8

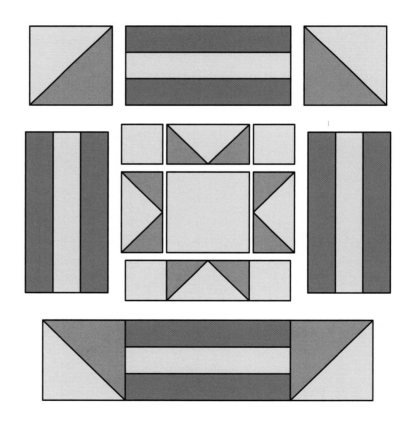

[101] STAR OF THE WEST

FINISHED BLOCK SIZE: 6" (15.2 CM) SQUARE

TEMPLATE NUMBERS & CUTTING
INSTRUCTIONS

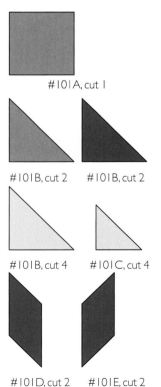

#101A, cut 1

#101B, cut 2   #101B, cut 2

#101B, cut 4   #101C, cut 4

#101D, cut 2   #101E, cut 2

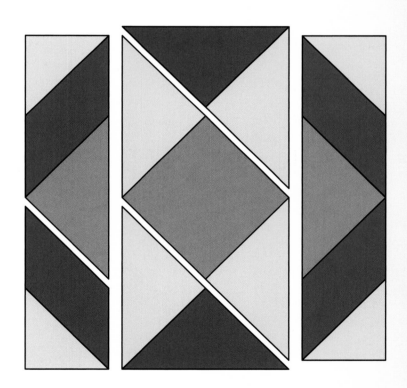

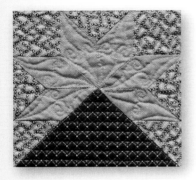

[102] STAR OVER THE MOUNTAIN

FINISHED BLOCK SIZE: 6" (15.2 CM) SQUARE

TEMPLATE NUMBERS & CUTTING INSTRUCTIONS

#102A, cut 1

#102B, cut 2

#102C, cut 6

#102D, cut 5

[103] SUMMER WINDS

FINISHED BLOCK SIZE: 6" (15.2 CM) SQUARE

TEMPLATE NUMBERS & CUTTING INSTRUCTIONS

#103A, cut 1

#103B, cut 4

#103C, cut 4

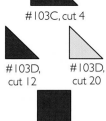

#103D, cut 12   #103D, cut 20

#103E, cut 4

[104] SUN RAY'S QUILT

FINISHED BLOCK SIZE: 6" (15.2 CM) SQUARE

TEMPLATE NUMBERS & CUTTING INSTRUCTIONS

#104A, cut 1

#104A, cut 4

#104B, cut 4

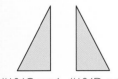

#104C, cut 4   #104D, cut 4

[105] SUNSHINY DAY

FINISHED BLOCK SIZE: 8" (20.3 CM) SQUARE

#105A, cut 4

#105B, cut 4

#105C, cut 4

#105D, cut 4

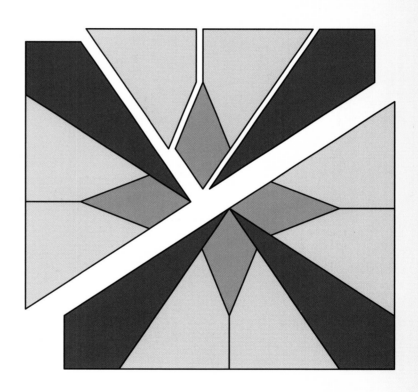

[106] TABLE FOR FOUR

FINISHED BLOCK SIZE: 8" (20.3 CM) SQUARE

TEMPLATE NUMBERS & CUTTING INSTRUCTIONS

 #106A, cut 4   #106A, cut 1

#106B, cut 8   #106B, cut 4

#106C, cut 4   #106C, cut 4

#106D, cut 4   #106D, cut 4

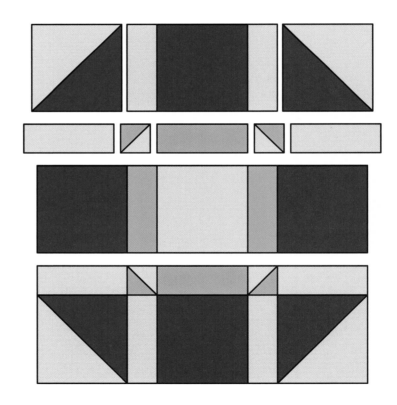

BLOCK ASSEMBLIES AND CUTTING INSTRUCTIONS

[107] TANGLED LINES

FINISHED BLOCK SIZE: 8" (20.3 CM) SQUARE

TEMPLATE NUMBERS & CUTTING INSTRUCTIONS

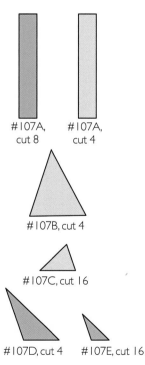

#107A, cut 8

#107A, cut 4

#107B, cut 4

#107C, cut 16

#107D, cut 4   #107E, cut 16

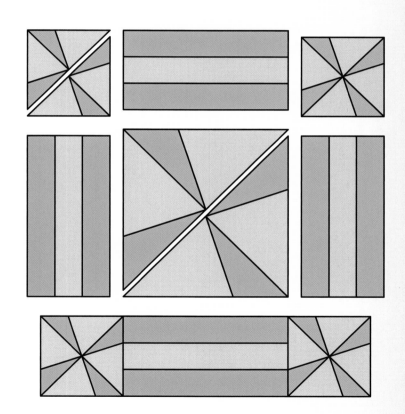

[108] TENDERFOOT

FINISHED BLOCK SIZE: 6" (15.2 CM) SQUARE

TEMPLATE NUMBERS & CUTTING INSTRUCTIONS

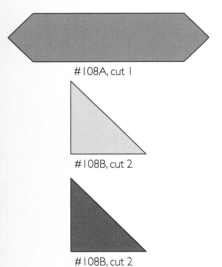

#108A, cut 1

#108B, cut 2

#108B, cut 2

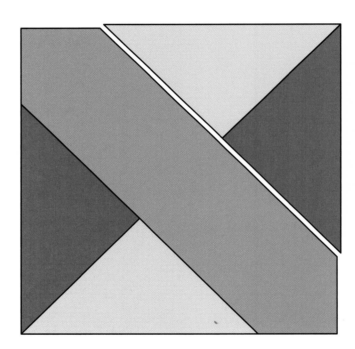

[109] THAT WILD COUNTRY

FINISHED BLOCK SIZE: 6" (15.2 CM) SQUARE

TEMPLATE NUMBERS & CUTTING INSTRUCTIONS

#109A, cut 2

#109A, cut 4

#109B, cut 2

#109C, cut 1   #109C, cut 2

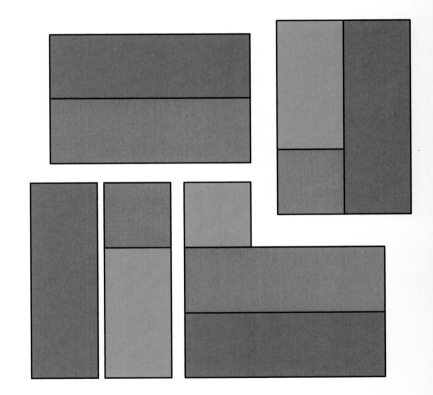

[110] THORNY THICKET

FINISHED BLOCK SIZE: 8" (20.3 CM) SQUARE

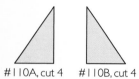

#110A, cut 4   #110B, cut 4

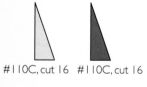

#110C, cut 16   #110C, cut 16

#110D, cut 4

#110E, cut 8   #110E, cut 8

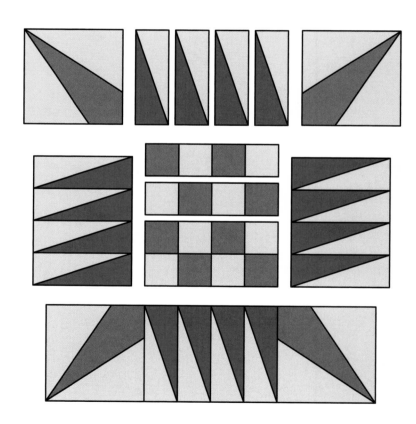

246

[111] TREASURED RECIPE

FINISHED BLOCK SIZE: 6" (15.2 CM) SQUARE

TEMPLATE NUMBERS & CUTTING
INSTRUCTIONS

#111A, cut 2

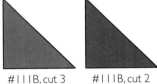

#111B, cut 3   #111B, cut 2

#111B, cut 1   #111C, cut 6

#111C, cut 2   #111C, cut 4

[112] TWISTED RIBBON

FINISHED BLOCK SIZE: 8" (20.3 CM) SQUARE

TEMPLATE NUMBERS & CUTTING INSTRUCTIONS

#112A, cut 1

#112B, cut 4

#112C, cut 4

#112C, cut 2

#112D, cut 2   #112E, cut 2

#112F, cut 4   #112F, cut 4   #112F, cut 4

#112G, cut 4   #112G, cut 12

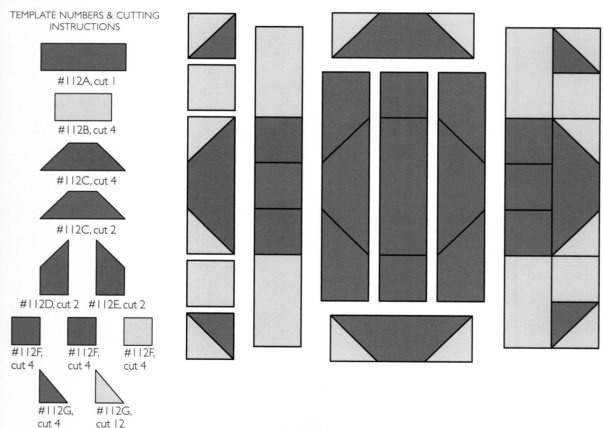

[113] UNREST EVERYWHERE

FINISHED BLOCK SIZE: 6" (15.2 CM) SQUARE

TEMPLATE NUMBERS & CUTTING INSTRUCTIONS

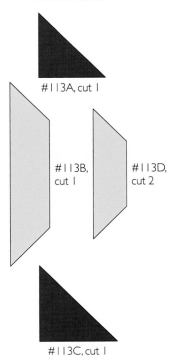

#113A, cut 1

#113B, cut 1

#113D, cut 2

#113C, cut 1

[114] UP ALL NIGHT

FINISHED BLOCK SIZE: 6" (15.2 CM) SQUARE

TEMPLATE NUMBERS & CUTTING INSTRUCTIONS

#114A, cut 4

#114B, cut 4

#114C, cut 4

#114D, cut 4

#114E, cut 4

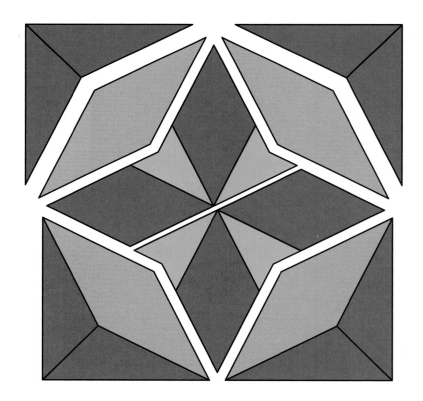

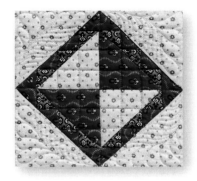

[115] VINES AT THE WINDOW

FINISHED BLOCK SIZE: 8" (20.3 CM) SQUARE

TEMPLATE NUMBERS & CUTTING
INSTRUCTIONS

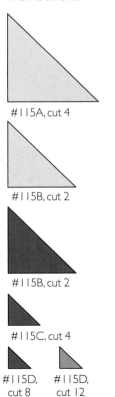

#115A, cut 4

#115B, cut 2

#115B, cut 2

#115C, cut 4

#115D,
cut 8

#115D,
cut 12

[116] WAGON WHEEL

FINISHED BLOCK SIZE: 8" (20.3 CM) SQUARE

TEMPLATE NUMBERS & CUTTING INSTRUCTIONS

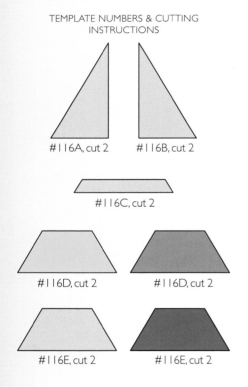

#116A, cut 2   #116B, cut 2

#116C, cut 2

#116D, cut 2   #116D, cut 2

#116E, cut 2   #116E, cut 2

[117] WATCHING THE CALENDAR

FINISHED BLOCK SIZE: 8" (20.3 CM) SQUARE

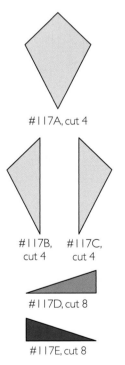

#117A, cut 4

#117B,   #117C,
cut 4   cut 4

#117D, cut 8

#117E, cut 8

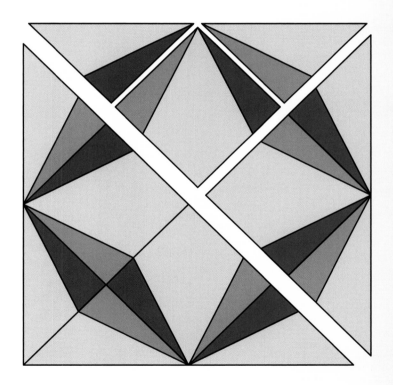

[118] WATER RICH

FINISHED BLOCK SIZE: 6" (15.2 CM) SQUARE

TEMPLATE NUMBERS & CUTTING INSTRUCTIONS

#118A, cut 4

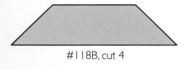

#118B, cut 4

#118C, cut 4

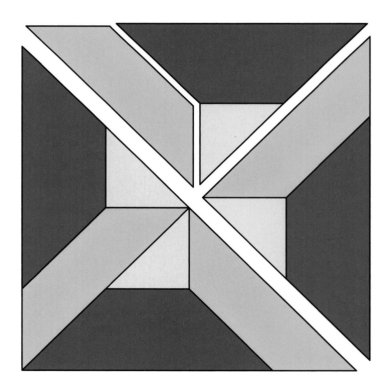

[119] WINDING TRAIL

FINISHED BLOCK SIZE: 8" (20.3 CM) SQUARE

TEMPLATE NUMBERS & CUTTING
INSTRUCTIONS

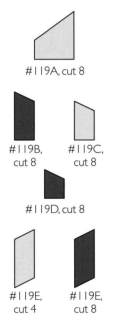

#119A, cut 8

#119B,
cut 8

#119C,
cut 8

#119D, cut 8

#119E,
cut 4

#119E,
cut 8

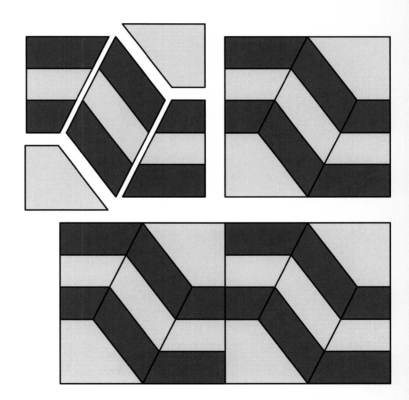

[120] WINDOW SQUARES

FINISHED BLOCK SIZE: 8" (20.3 CM) SQUARE

TEMPLATE NUMBERS & CUTTING INSTRUCTIONS

#120A, cut 4

#120B, cut 4

#120C, cut 1

#120D, cut 4   #120E, cut 4

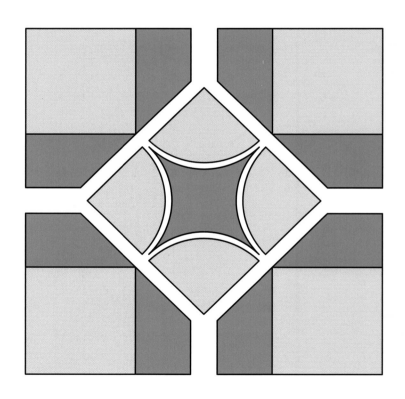

[121] WINTER'S NIGHT

FINISHED BLOCK SIZE: 8" (20.3 CM) SQUARE

TEMPLATE NUMBERS & CUTTING INSTRUCTIONS

#121A, cut 8

#121A, cut 8

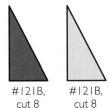

#121B, cut 8   #121B, cut 8

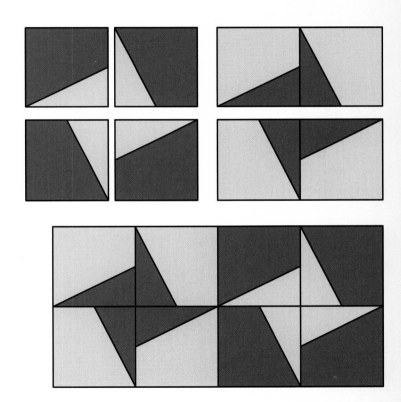

The Quilt Assembly Instructions

Quilt Assembly

Directions for the queen-size quilt can be found in steps 1–13 below, and on pages 262–265.
Directions for the lap-size quilt are found in steps 1–5 and 14–15 below, and on pages 266–268.
This quilt is built from the center medallion block out. Sew the fabric strips and block units
in numerical order following the quilt assembly diagrams.

QUILT TOP ASSEMBLY

1. Begin with the center 18" (45.7 cm) Rising Sun [#93] block. Sew border #1 to the top and bottom of the block. Then sew border #2 to the left and right sides of the center block.

2. For borders #3 and #4, piece four Flying Geese borders, using the diagram for orientation. Sew together ten Flying Geese units each for the top and bottom borders and fourteen Flying Geese units each for the left and right side borders. Sew the 10-unit Flying Geese borders to the top and bottom of the center unit and the 14-unit Flying Geese borders to the left and right sides.

3. Sew the #5 borders to the top and bottom. Sew the #6 borders to the left and right sides.

4. For block borders #7 and #8, sew together four 8" (20.3 cm) blocks each for the top and bottom border; make 2 units. Sew together six 8" (20.3 cm) blocks each for the left and right sides; make 2 units. Sew the 4-block units to the top and bottom of the quilt top, then sew the 6-block units to the left and right sides.

5. Add the next round of border strips. Sew the #9 border to the top and bottom; then sew the #10 border to the left and right sides.

Note: Skip to Step 14 if you are making the lap-size quilt.

6. Sew together eight 6" (15.2 cm) blocks for borders #11 and #12; make 4 units. Sew one block border to the top and one block border to the bottom of the quilt. Sew one 2½" × 6" (6.4cm × 15.2 cm) strip to the top of a block; make 2. Sew one strip to the bottom of a block; make 2. Attach these units to the top and bottom ends of the remaining two 8-unit block borders. Attach to the left and right sides of the quilt top.

7. Sew borders #13 to the top and bottom of the quilt top. Sew borders #14 to the left and right sides.

8. For borders #15 and #16, sew together four 8" (20.3 cm) blocks; make 4 units. Sew together five 8" (20.3 cm) blocks; make 4 units. Sew together four Flying Geese; make 4 units total. To make the top and bottom #14 pieced block borders, sew together in this order:

one 4-block unit, one Flying Geese unit and one 4-block unit. Make 2. For the left and right #15 side borders, sew together in this order: one 5-block unit, one Flying Geese unit and one 5-block unit; Make 2. Sew the 8-block pieced borders to the top and bottom of the quilt. Sew the 10-block pieced borders to the left and right sides.

9. Sew border strip #17 the top and bottom of the quilt.

10. For block border #18, sew together fourteen 6" (15.2 cm) blocks. Make 2. Sew them to the top and bottom of the quilt.

11. Sew #19 border strips to the top and bottom of the quilt top. Sew #20 to the left and right sides.

12. For pieced borders #21 and #22, sew (186) Template B blocks. Make (2) 43-block strips and (2) 53-block strips. See the Assembly Diagram for block orientation. Sew the 43-block border strips to the top and bottom of the quilt; sew the 53-block border strips to the left and right sides.

13. Sew the #23 border strips to the top and bottom; sew the #24 border strips to the left and right sides.

14. Continuing the directions for the lap-size quilt. For pieced borders #11 and #12, sew 104 Template B blocks. Make two 25-block strips and two 27-block strips. See the Assembly Diagram for block orientation.

Sew the 25-block border strips to the top and bottom of the quilt; sew the 27-block strips to the left and right sides.

15. Sew the #13 border strips to the top and bottom; sew #14 border strips to the left and right sides.

FINISHING THE QUILT

16. Piece the backing fabric to make a back that is 4" (10.2 cm) larger than the quilt top on each side.

17. Layer the quilt sandwich by placing the backing on the floor, right side down. Tape in place with low-tack tape, making sure the backing is flat but not too taut.

18. Place the batting over the backing, ensuring the batting is at least 2" (5 cm) larger than the top on each side. Then center the quilt top right side up over the batting.

19. Baste or pin the layers together, then quilt as desired.

20. Sew the binding strips together end to end. Sew the binding on using your preferred method.

QUILT ASSEMBLY INSTRUCTIONS

Queen-Size Quilt

There are 121 blocks in the queen-size quilt—sixty-four 6" (15.2 cm), fifty-six 8" (20.3 cm) blocks, and an 18" (45.7 cm) center medallion block.

FINISHED QUILT SIZE
94" × 110" (238.8 cm × 279.4 cm)

FINISHED BLOCK SIZES

- (64) 6" (15.2 cm) square
- (56) 8" (20.3 cm) square
- (1) 18" (45.7 cm) square
- (192) 2" × 2" (4.8 cm × 4.8 cm) border units
- (64) 2" × 4" (4.8 cm × 10 cm) flying geese units

FABRIC REQUIREMENTS

- Border and binding fabric, 3⅝ yards (2.3 m)
- Backing fabric, 8¾ yards (8 m) of 42–44" (111.8 cm), seams set horizontally
- Batting, 3⅜ yards (23 m) of 108" (274.3 cm) batting, set lengthwise or 3 yards (2.7 m) of 120" (304.8 cm) wide batting, or 2 queen-sized batts, seamed horizontally.

CUTTING LIST

Note: Based on 40" (101.6 cm) width of fabric. Number and label the fabric strips before you begin. To compensate for any small discrepancies in length, it's recommended that you measure your quilt at each stage before cutting the next border strips. Keep in mind that I have listed the ideal measurements and although a little deviation is acceptable, too much will cause difficulties when attaching the next round of borders.

- (2) 18½" × 1½" (47 cm × 3.8 cm) strips for top border and bottom (strip 1)
- (2) 20½" × 1½" (52.1 × 3.8 cm) strips left and right (strip 2)
- (2) 28½" × 2½" (72.4 cm × 6.4 cm) strips for top and bottom borders (strip 5)
- (2) 32½" × 2½" (82.6 cm × 6.4 cm) strips for left and right (strip 6)
- (2) 48½" × 2½" (123.2 cm × 6.4 cm) strips for top and bottom borders (strip 9)
- (2) 64½" × 2½" (163.8 cm × 6.4 cm) strips for left and right side borders (strip 10)
- (4) 6½" × 2½" (16.5 cm × 6.4 cm) strips for left and right sides (strip 12)

- (2) 64½" × 2½" (163.8 cm × 6.4 cm) strips for top and bottom borders (strip 13)
- (2) 68½" × 2½" (174 cm × 6.4 cm) strips for left and right side borders (strip 14)
- (2) 84½" × 2½" (214.6 cm × 6.4 cm) top and bottom (strip 17)
- (2) 84½" × 1½" (214.6 cm × 3.8 cm) strips for top and bottom borders (strip 19)
- (2) 102½" × 1½" (260.4 cm × 3.8 cm) strips for left and right side borders (strip 20)
- (2) 90½" × 2 ½" (229.9 cm × 6.4 cm) strips for top and bottom borders (strip 23)
- (2) 110½" × 2 ½" (280.7 cm × 6.4 cm) strips for left and right side borders (strip 24)
- (11) 2½" × 40" (6.4 cm × 101.6 cm) strips for binding

QUEEN QUILT MAP

B ... B

| 26 | 82 | 29 | 33 | 5 | 81 | 91 | 28 | 59 | 97 | 101 | 74 | 37 | 22 |

| 35 | 75 | 66 | 57 | 54 | A | 96 | 85 | 24 | 58 | 45 |

B

106 | 10 | 14 | 108 | 89 | 95 | 118 | 104 | 64 | 32 | 12 | 16 | B

105 | 47 | 117 | 112 | 92 | 70 | 53 | 76 | 6 | 119

68 | 2 / 15 | 71 | A | 19 | 83 / 36 | 67

23 | 8 | 4 | A 93 A | 52 | 41 | 7

A | 86 | 30 | | 99 | A

43 | 90 | 31 | A | 49 | 9 / 102 | 38

116 | 34 | 121 | 110 | 100 | 120 | 44 | 13 | 18 | 21

115 | 72 | 69 | 46

B | 79 | 3 | 109 | 84 | 17 | 25 | 1 | 42 | 103 | 62 | 65 | B

| 27 | 39 | 56 | 60 | 63 | A | 11 | 78 | 98 | 48 | 80 |

| 87 | 51 | 50 | 77 | 73 | 114 | 61 | 40 | 20 | 94 | 113 | 55 | 111 | 88 |

B ... B

QUILT ASSEMBLY INSTRUCTIONS

263

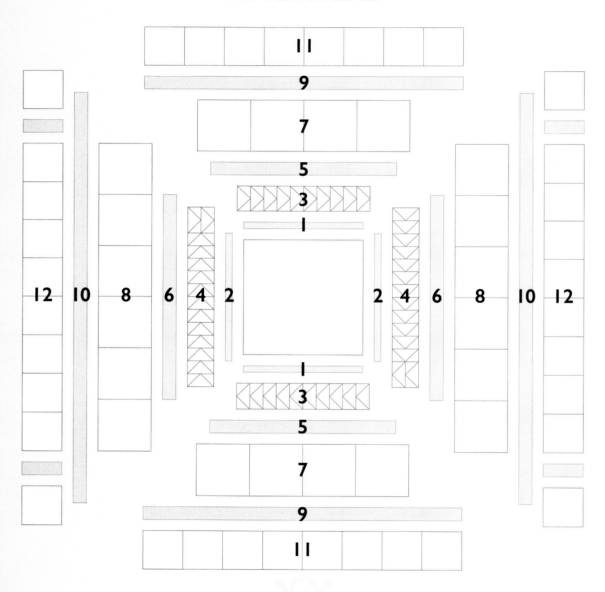

QUILT ASSEMBLY INSTRUCTIONS

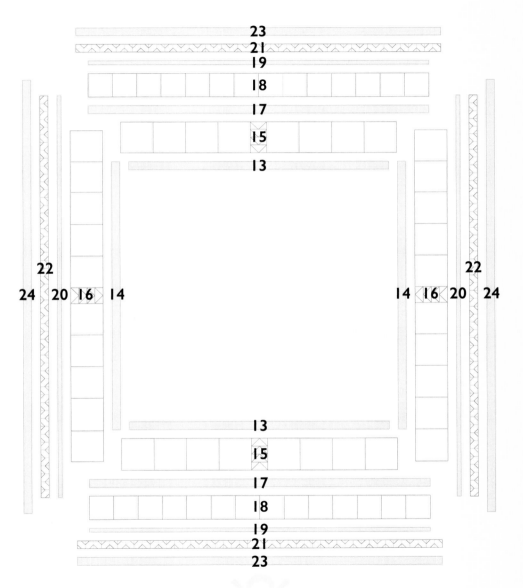

Lap-Size Quilt

Pick 20 of your favorite 8" (20.3 cm) blocks to go with the 18" (45.7 cm)
#93 Rising Sun, Variation block to make this lap-size quilt.

FINISHED QUILT SIZE
58" (147.3 cm) square

FINISHED BLOCK SIZES

- (20) 8" (20.3 cm) square
- (1) 18" (45.7 cm) square
- (104) 2" (5 cm) square (template B)
- (48) 2" × 4" (5 cm × 10 cm) Flying Geese units

FABRIC REQUIREMENTS

- Border and binding fabric, 1⅝ yards (1.5 m)
- Backing fabric, 3⅝ yards (3.3 m) of 42–44" (111.8 cm) wide fabric
- Batting, 1⅞ yards (1.6 m) of 90" (228.6 cm) wide batting

CUTTING LIST

Note: Based on 40" (101.6 cm) width of fabric. Number and label the fabric strips before you begin.
To compensate for any small discrepancies in length, it's recommended that you measure your quilt at each stage before cutting the next border strips. Keep in mind that I have listed the ideal measurements and although a little deviation is acceptable, too much will cause difficulties when attaching the next round of borders.

- (2) 18½" × 1½" (47cm × 3.8 cm) strips for top and bottom (strip 1)
- (2) 20½" × 1½" (52.1 cm × 3.8 cm) strips for left and right sides (strip 2)
- (2) 28½" × 2½" (72.4 cm × 6.4 cm) strips for top and bottom (strip 5)
- (2) 32½" × 2½" (82.6 cm × 6.4 cm) strips for left and right side (strip 6)

- (2) 48½" × 1½" (123 cm × 3.8 cm) for top and bottom (strip 9)
- (2) 50½" × 1½" (128.3 cm × 3.8 cm) for left and right side (strip 10)
- (2) 54½" × 2½" (138.4 cm × 6.4 cm) strips for top and bottom (strip 13)
- (2) 58½" × 2½" (148.6 cm × 6.4 cm) strips for left and right sides (strip 14)

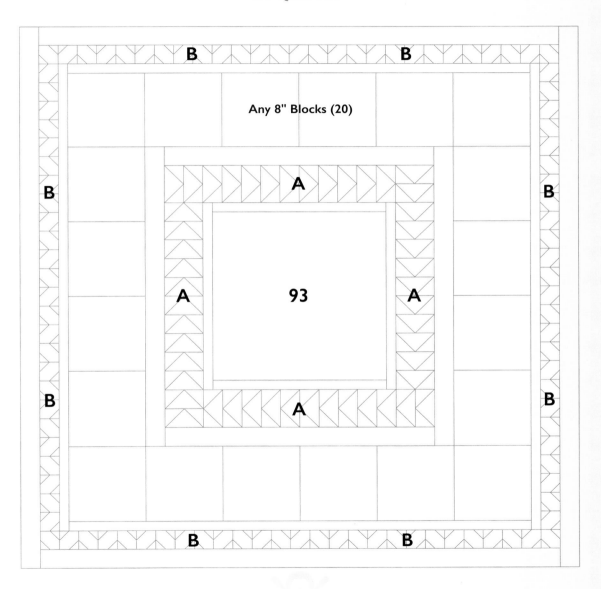

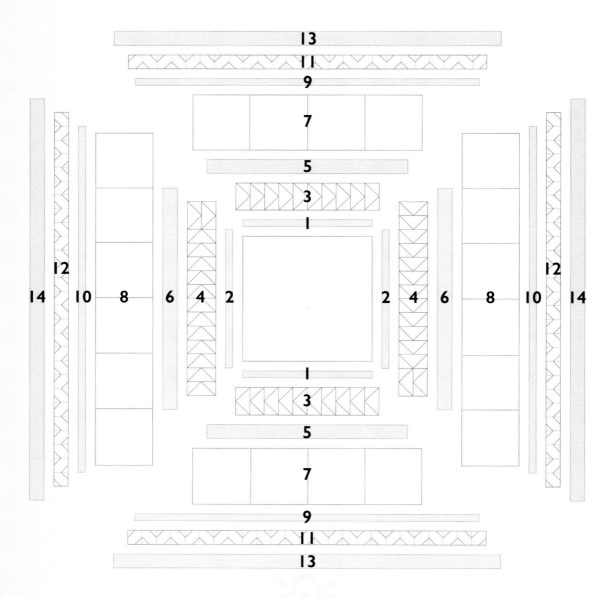

QUILT ASSEMBLY INSTRUCTIONS

Index

METRIC CONVERSION CHART

TO CONVERT	TO	MULTIPLY BY
INCHES	CENTIMETERS	2.54
CENTIMETERS	INCHES	0.4
FEET	CENTIMETERS	30.5
CENTIMETERS	FEET	0.03
YARDS	METERS	0.9
METERS	YARDS	1.1

About the Author

DEDICATION

IN REMEMBRANCE OF Ada...

When I reach that land of promise,

Sweeter strains my lips shall frame,

But the theme will still be Jesus,

Glory! Glory! To His name!

From the hymn, All the Day, *1900,*
by Ada Melville Shaw

LAURIE AARON HIRD enjoys quilting, embroidery, and her porch view of the countryside from her home in the great Midwest. She is the author of *The Bible Sampler Quilt* and three other books in *The Farmer's Wife Quilt* series.

ACKNOWLEDGMENTS

I wish to thank—Peg Ries, of Epworth, Iowa, for longarm quilting Ada's quilt. Peg's work is gorgeous, and I could not be more pleased and thankful that she chose to share her skill with me again. Janet Stiles, for graciously helping me in my research of the homestead church that Ada attended. Jill Shaulis, of Yellow Creek Quilt Designs, Pearl City, Illinois, for the surprise gift of a fat quarter bundle of her Windham's Kindred Spirits II fabrics. The entire production team at F+W Media for their expert assistance in producing this book, with special thanks Maya Elson, Jodi Butler, Debra Greenway, and Kerry Bogert. And to Nancy for her love and kindness.